Y0-BRD-476

DEAR
Muslim
FRIEND

JERRY MATTIX

ECS
MINISTRIES
The Word to the World

Dear Muslim Friend

Jerry Mattix

Published by:
    ECS Ministries
    PO Box 1028
    Dubuque, IA 52004-1028
    phone: (563) 585-2070
    email: ecsorders@ecsministries.org
    website: www.ecsministries.org

First Printed 2014

ISBN 978-1-59387-219-9

Code: B-DMF

Copyright © 2014 ECS Ministries

All rights reserved. No part of this publication may be
reproduced or transmitted in any manner, electronic
or mechanical, including photocopy, recording, or any
information storage and retrieval system including the
Internet without written permission from the publisher.
Permission is not needed for brief quotations embodied in
critical articles and reviews.

Jonah illustration on page 43 © Robert T. Barrett
(www.roberttbarrett.com). All rights reserved.

Cover design by Amy Schiltz.

All Scripture quotations, unless otherwise indicated, are
taken from The Holy Bible, English Standard Version®
(ESV®), copyright © 2001 by Crossway Bibles, a
publishing ministry of Good News Publishers. Used by
permission. All rights reserved.

Printed in the United States of America

What's Included In This Book

Arabic Words Used:

Dawut – David

Habil – Abel

Hawwa – Eve

Iblis – Satan

Ibrahim – Abraham

imam – muslim cleric

Injil – New Testament

Isa – Jesus

Isa al Masih – Jesus Christ

Jebril – Gabriel

Kafir – Infidels

Kalamullah – Word of God

Maryam – Mary

Musa – Moses

Qabil – Cain

Ruhul Qudus – Holy Spirit

shirk – the sin of associating anyone with God

surah – chapter of the Koran

tahrif – alteration

Tawrat – Books of Moses

Yahya – John the Baptist

Zabur – Books of History (David)

A Letter to My Friends

Dear Muslim Friend,

I greet you in the name of the one true God, who created the whole Universe. We may believe differently about God and His revelation, but He is still the one and only Creator of us all. We may have been born in different countries with different ideas about God, however I believe that it is the responsibility of every one of us to seek to know the one true God. Because, in the end, it is not where we were born that decides our fate or future, but rather our correct understanding and belief in the one true God.

> It is not where we were born that decides our fate or future, but rather our correct understanding and belief in the one true God.

Many people think that our place of birth and family determine our religion. I do not believe this is true. In fact when I talk with people and they tell me their religion, I always ask them: "Why do you believe that way?" Whether they are Christian or Muslim they often struggle to find

5

an answer and finally admit that the only reason they consider themselves Christian or Muslim is because they were born or raised in such a family. Then I ask them: "Does it make sense for our eternal destiny to be based simply on where we were born or what family we were raised in? If that is true, then how will God judge the animist, who is born in some far corner of the world with no true knowledge of God? Is he doomed to be a pagan simply because he was born there?" Certainly not!

I was born and raised in a Christian family. I went to church since I was a child but in my early teens I began to be fearful of death and hell. I realized that if I died and had to stand before the great Judge of the Universe and that if He asked me why I should be delivered from hell fire, I really didn't have a good answer. If I claimed to be a Christian, He would ask me why. And the only answer I had was to say that my parents were Christians. Even at that age, I knew that answer was not good enough. So I realized that I had to research for myself and make a personal decision about my faith in God. It was only after reading God's Word, the Bible, for myself that I found peace in my soul and freedom from fear.

I believe that every one of us has the same responsibility to search for the truth. If we are Christians simply because we grew up in America or Europe going to church or if we are Muslims simply because we grew up in the Middle East going to the mosque this will not save us in the Last Day. Faith and religion is a personal choice. We cannot simply assume that we were born with the right religion. We must search for the truth. There is only one God, so I believe there is only one way to God. Which way is it? How can I be sure that the faith of my fathers is the truth? We can only know for certain if we search for the truth and choose to believe it for ourselves. Only the truth will set us free and lead us to a true knowledge of God and salvation from hell.

> We cannot simply assume that we were born with the right religion. We must search for the truth.

I have lived for many years in the Middle East discussing this important subject with my many Muslim friends. Unlike most Westerners, Middle Easterners understand that religion is important to all of life and I have found that most are eager to talk with me. And yet I have also found that many of them believe that just calling themselves Muslims is enough. I don't believe this is true for either those who call themselves Muslims or for those who call themselves Christians. Knowing the truth and talking about it is not enough; we must also practice the truth in our daily lives. Empty talk does not trick God.

Another thing that I find in talking with my many Muslim friends and Christian friends is that they don't have accurate information about the other person's religion or even about their own. They think they know what Christians believe, but in reality they only know what others have told them. Although they claim to believe in Isa and the Injil, most have never read it for themselves. In fact I have found that many have not even read the Qur'an but only know what they have been taught or heard from others. I remind them that the opinions or faith of others will not save them. That is why I believe that reading God's Word and learning the facts for ourselves is critical.

> God has given each and every one of us a mind to search and a heart to believe.

It is sad but true that most of us have simply trusted what "religious" people have told us about God without investigating for ourselves. And yet, if God only wanted the imams and priests to read and understand the holy books then He would only have given brains to priests and imams! But we know that God has given each and every one of us a mind to search and a heart to believe. In the Last Day when God judges mankind, we will each be judged individually for our own actions. We will have to answer for ourselves. That is why we must be certain of the truth. We cannot simply trust that we are right just because our parents or religious teachers told us, since they probably only believed because their parents told them so. We must go to the root of the matter and examine the sources for ourselves. Only then will we know how to answer our Creator and Judge.

Isa al Masih said: *"If you know the truth, it will set you free"* (John 8:32). We all want freedom but unfortunately many are afraid to really search for the truth. And yet only knowledge of the truth will give us true freedom. When I challenge my Muslim friends to study the Qur'an or Injil for themselves they often hesitate because they are afraid it might confuse them. I remind them that if God truly loves us and cares about our future then He will surely reveal His truth to us. God is not a God of confusion; He is light and truth. In fact, I have often told my friends that if someone convinces me that I do not have the whole truth and shows me what the full truth is, instead of being angry I should gladly thank them and embrace the truth even if it is different from what I knew before. Ultimately it is not important that I prove my religion right or your religion wrong: what is important is knowing the truth about God.

> God is not a God of confusion; He is light and truth.

My dear friend, each one of us has grown up with different ideas about God. Whether we like it or not we all have prejudices. However the fact is that this life is passing and soon we will all give account of ourselves to God. It is time to search for the truth and know what we believe. We can no longer assume that only we are right and that everyone else is wrong. We must go to the holy books with our questions and not stop until we find answers. Most importantly we must trust that the great and only God is willing and able to show us the truth if we seek Him with sincerity. So now before you continue reading, I urge you to take a moment and open your heart to God. Pray to Him, He is always listening. Ask Him to show you His truth and His love.

I have included here some of the most common questions that my Muslim friends have asked me about my beliefs and I have tried to answer them directly from the sources. I believe that God loves us all the same and that He is eager to guide everyone who sincerely seeks Him to know the truth. You may have some fears but I beg you to put them aside and trust that God will open your eyes to the truth and show you His way.

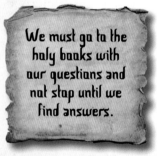

We must go to the holy books with our questions and not stop until we find answers.

Why Conflict?

In discussing my beliefs with my Muslim friends I usually find that they have a negative view of my faith. This is not because they are intolerant or unloving people. On the contrary, I have found Middle Eastern people to be incredibly hospitable and eager to talk about religious matters. Most often the reason for this negative opinion of my faith is their lack of accurate information regarding Christianity and/or their misunderstanding of who are true Christians and of what we actually believe.

This misunderstanding and misinformation goes both directions. Just as Muslims often do not understand our beliefs or accurately represent Christians, Christians have often made the same mistake in misrepresenting Islam and believing that all Muslims are evil. I believe the real root of these misunderstandings—on both sides—stems from the lack of accurate information and respectful dialogue about each other's cultural and religious values.

At the root of these problems lies a more general misconception. Most Muslims I have met believe that the "West" is Christian. They believe this mainly because their countries in the "East" are largely Muslim and are in some cases ruled according to various interpretations of the Sharia Law. So their natural assumption is that all countries to the west of them, since they are not Muslim, must be "Christian" and/or ruled by Biblical laws. Although those in the West know this is not true, it is important to understand the practical results of this simple misconception. From a Muslim perspective this means that everything that takes place in Western "Christian" countries, is done by Christians living according to the Bible. For example, all that comes out of Hollywood is viewed as representative of Christian beliefs. Muslims do not realize that true Christians in the West are just as opposed as they are to the gross immorality so prominent in Western media and society.

Here is another example: when Western countries decide to wage war on a Middle Eastern country Muslims think this is a religious conflict, a Christian war against Islam. Again they are not aware that many Western governments are secular governments that don't necessarily follow Christian beliefs or values. In fact most of my Muslim friends are shocked to find out that the majority of the "West" is not Christian. Or, that the vast majority in traditionally "Christian" European countries like Denmark or France are in fact agnostic or atheistic, meaning they don't believe in God at all and even the few that still claim to be Christian are not always following Isa al Masih in their daily lives. Of course the media in both the East and the West play a large role in promoting this prejudice and creating more confusion. So in order to break down these misconceptions and understand one another, we must learn the facts about each other's religions. For this we need to go back to the actual source and roots of our religious beliefs and values.

We must learn the facts about each other's religions.

In the following pages we will touch on the most important points of contention between Christianity and Islam. My hope and prayer is that this book will be used by God to help tear down the wall of misconceptions that continue to divide East and West, and that we might be united in the knowledge of the truth.

Is the Bible
(Tawrat, Zabur, Injil)
Trustworthy?

One of the most important questions we must deal with right away is whether or not we can trust the Injil as the Word of God. All Muslims agree that the Injil came from God, but many claim that the Injil has been changed or corrupted by various "priests" down through history. Perhaps you think this as well. First of all, it should be stated that to this day no one has been able to support this claim with any real evidence. Every one of these claims is based on what others say, people's opinions, and has no foundation. Everyone has opinions about almost everything, but very often they are not correct.

Some people confidently claim that the original Injil revealed to Isa was lost early on, and that Christians today use a fabricated version. However, when asked the following questions, they are unable to provide solid answers:

> Have you seen any evidence that today's Injil was changed?

- Could you show us exactly where it was changed?

- If the current Injil is a fabrication where is the real one?

- Why would Christians want to change their holy book?

- How could God allow people to corrupt His Word?

The response to these questions is usually something like this; "I don't know, I just heard that it was so . . ." It is unfortunate that so much of what people think they know about Christianity is simply based on rumors and other people's opinions.

The truth is that the Injil has not been changed or falsified. When all the available evidence for the text and history of the Injil is examined, using modern scientific methods

The Injil has not been changed or falsified.

and common logic, we are faced with clear evidence that the Injil is God's revelation, which has remained unchanged from the time it was written and has reached us in its entirety. Let's look at some of the evidence and at other important questions raised by this false claim that the Injil has been corrupted.

Can the Almighty God Not Protect His Word?

My dear Muslim friend, we must realize that if we believe the claims made above, then we are in effect doubting God's wisdom, His truth, and power and thus insulting His character. After all, we believe in the one God who is almighty and unchanging. Since God is in fact the same yesterday, today, and forever, then His Word is likewise unchangeable. Since He revealed His Word to humanity, He must have the power to protect His Word as well. If God cannot preserve His own Word, how can He prove Himself trustworthy on anything? When people speak this way of God's Word, I remind them that they are not putting Christianity on trial but rather they are putting God and His holy character on trial.

To claim that God's Word has changed or was lost is in fact to claim that God has no honor.

In Middle Eastern culture, it is essential that a person be true to their word, because our words are a reflection of our character. If one does not keep his word then he has no honor. To break your word is the ultimate shame and dishonor. In this instance, if God cannot keep His Word, what would happen to His honor? To claim that God's Word has changed or was lost is in fact to claim that God has no honor. God forbid!

To this many of my Muslim friends respond that it was not God who changed His Word, but rather corrupt priests. If this is the case, then we would be saying that some corrupt priests were more powerful than God. Is that possible? Also if God is all-powerful and all-knowing, then when he revealed the Injil wouldn't He have known from the beginning that it would be corrupted by men? On the contrary, God has promised in the Bible that His holy Word will not pass away but will in fact remain forever:

- ❖ *Forever, O Lord, Your Word is firmly fixed in the heavens* (Psalm 119:89).

- ❖ *Heaven and earth will pass away, but My words will not pass away* (Matthew 24:35).

- ❖ *Since you have been born again, not of perishable seed but of imperishable, through the living and abiding word of God; for all flesh is like grass and all its glory like the flower of grass. The grass withers, and the flower falls, but the Word of the Lord remains forever* (1 Peter 1:23-25).[1]

Actually, the claim that the Injil has been changed is simply not possible or even logical. Let's say that there was some priest who lived 500 years after Isa who didn't agree with certain teachings in the Injil so he set out to change the text. In order to succeed he would have had to collect all of the thousands of written copies of

---

[1] See also: Matthew 5:17-19; John 10:35.

the Injil in Greek that had been distributed throughout the world, as well as the hundreds of translations that have been made by that time, then he would have to rewrite them one by one before sending them out again. Do you think this would be possible for even a whole group of priests? Of course not!

Now suppose for a moment that God allowed men to change the Injil. Then on judgment day when a Christian who believed in Isa and the Injil and was martyred for his cause stands before God, what do you think God will say: "Sorry my friend, the book you believed in and died for was corrupted." If God allowed His Word to be changed by men then how could He judge mankind? Clearly it is essential that God's Word does not change because ultimately He will judge this world by His Word.

The idea that the Injil was changed is not actually taught in the Muslim sacred text the Qur'an.

It is important for you to know that the idea that the Injil was changed (*tahrif*) is not actually taught in the Muslim sacred text the Qur'an.[2] On the contrary, the Qur'an testifies to the fact that God's words cannot be changed (Al-An'am 6:34, 115; Yunus 10:64). Muslims are likewise commanded to accept the Tawrat,

---

[2] Steer, Malcolm *A Muslim's Pocket Guide to Christianity* (Christian Focus, 2005) 42.

Zabur, and Injil as God's words and threatened with punishment if they refuse (An-Nisa 4:136-138, Ghafir 40:70-72). In another passage Muslims are commanded to consult "the people of the book" (Ahl al-Kitab) if they are in doubt about what their book teaches (Yunus 10:94). It is clear from these passages that the Bible was accepted as God's Word by Muslims in the time of Muhammad.[3] Now there are some verses in the Qur'an that seem to imply that the teachings of the Bible might have been tampered with,[4] but upon closer examination it is clear that this is only speaking of people who misinterpret the holy text.[5] The idea that the Injil was changed is foreign to the Qur'an and became popular only many centuries after it was written.

Is There Any Historic/Textual Evidence for the Injil?

God had given each of us not only a heart to believe but also minds to search and understand. God does not expect us to blindly believe in His Word, but rather He encourages us to use the minds He has given us to logically research the truth. So as we seek to find if the Injil is reliable, we can also look to historical and archeological evidence.

---

[3] Bramsen, P.D. *One God One Message* (www.rockintl.org, 2007) 29-31.
[4] See: Al Maidah 5:13; Ali Imran 3:78.
[5] Shlemon, Alan *The Ambassadors Guide to Islam* (www.str. org, 2010) 18-21.

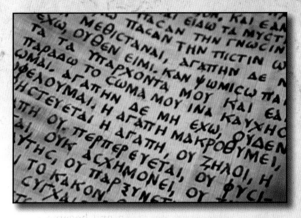

Greek Manuscript of 1st Corinthians 13

What you will find is that there are thousands of ancient Injil manuscripts displayed in archeological museums throughout the world, which readily prove that the Injil was never changed. Beginning from the second century AD, there are more than 5,300 hand-written Greek manuscripts, that is, ancient copies of the Injil.[6] But that is not all. There are over 10,000 ancient Latin manuscripts. There are also more than 9,300 ancient hand-written translations of the Injil into other languages like Coptic, Chaldean, Syriac, and others, many of which date back to shortly after the time of Isa. Furthermore, the early Church Fathers made roughly 24,000 quotations from the Injil in their theological

---

[6] Geisler, Norman and Saleeb, Abdul, *Answering Islam* (Grand Rapids, Baker Book House, 2002) 213.

books and writings, so much so that almost the entire Injil could be reconstructed from their quotations alone.[7] This shows that there is overwhelming textual evidence that the Injil has been miraculously preserved by God.

Today when the Injil is translated into any language, it is done from the original Greek text, which has been compiled by scholars who have compared thousands of ancient Injil manuscripts. It is interesting that none of the classic ancient Greek manuscripts, such as Homer's Iliad or Plato's works, has even five percent of the textual evidence that the Injil has—not to mention the fact that the oldest manuscript of the Iliad was written 500 years after Homer.[8] And yet when it comes to the Injil we have some copies written as early as 100 years after Isa and some even earlier fragments. The fact is that throughout history there has been no other book that has been as well preserved with such abundant evidence as the Injil.

Despite all this evidence, some people claim that there are thousands of "errors" in the Injil manuscripts. To what are they referring? Well, naturally among so many thousands of ancient copies there are small variations. And yet when the texts are compared with one another, scholars are able to see where words were misspelled or when letters were added. So after careful comparison and analysis they can be certain of the original text.

---

[7] McDowell, Josh, A Ready Defense (Nashville, Thomas Publishers, 1993) 43.

I think it is also reasonable to expect that, if any significant changes had actually been made, then the content of the Injil itself would reflect this, since this would cause major discrepancies in the text. In other words, as we read the Injil we would find all kinds of contradictions. Furthermore it would be impossible for the thousands of manuscripts to be in agreement with each other. But as it is, everyone who studies the Injil can see for himself just how consistent and complete it is.

There are others who claim that there are contradictions in the Injil. But often, what appears to be an error or contradiction comes from misinterpreting the text or the culture in which the Injil was written. What we often find is that two verses that might initially seem to be contradictory actually complement and support one another by providing different perspectives.[9]

One fourth of the Bible speaks about future events.

Over the years I have challenged many of my friends to show me real errors in the Injil but none has succeeded. It is in fact the Bible's absolute accuracy with regard to history, science, and even the future that strengthens our confidence in God's Word.

---

8 See: Geisler and Saleeb, 232-233.
9 See: Bramsen, 23-24.

What the Bible says about the future is especially significant. Many are not aware of the fact that almost one fourth of the Bible speaks about future events.[10] These are not simply good guesses or general predictions about future events either. On the contrary, the Bible gives the names of some famous emperors and speaks of their achievements in great detail hundreds of years before they were born.[11] More importantly, there are hundreds of predictions about the coming of Isa al Masih. No other book in human history contains this many bold prophecies about the future. And many of them are being fulfilled even in our day and age.[12] These Bible prophecies serve as God's fingerprints on human history to remind us that He is in control and that His Word, the Bible, is in fact true and unchanged.

God's Word, the Bible, has never been changed and cannot be changed.

Because of our faith in the unchanging character of God and because of historical evidence, we can say with confidence that God's Word, the Bible, has never been changed and cannot be changed.

---

[10] Tim Lahaye and Jerry Jenkins, *Are we living in the end Times* (Tyndale, 2011) pg. 3
[11] See: Isaiah 44:28; Daniel 11
[12] See: Matthew 24

Were Four Injils Chosen
at the Council of Nicea?

Another widespread claim is that in AD 325 at the Council of Nicea, only four Injils (Matthew, Mark, Luke and John) were selected from among thousands of other manuscripts. I've often been told a rather humorous story concerning how the four Injils were chosen. It goes like this: "Christian religious leaders heaped hundreds of Injils onto a table, which was then shaken vigorously. All the books tumbled off the table on to the floor except for four manuscripts. The four books left on the table were Matthew, Mark, Luke and John, which were then accepted as the genuine Injils." In this story, they claim, that the beliefs of the entire Christian world were determined by shaking a table!

The fact is that the historical evidence about the Council of Nicea contradicts such absurd claims. Just looking at the Injil used by Christians today disproves this tale, because we all use one Injil, not four versions. The books Matthew, Mark, Luke and John are in fact only the first four sections of the total 27 sections or books which make up the entire Injil. The Qur'an is likewise composed of 114 surahs but that does not mean there are 114 Qur'ans. As discussed before, when we evaluate the true historical sources we can see that there has never been another universally accepted Injil. Likewise the Injil used by Christians all over the world today is one and the same book.

It might be helpful to clarify here exactly how the Injil was revealed to mankind. Most of my Muslim friends assume that it was delivered in its entirety to Isa much like the Qur'an was revealed to Muhammad in visions. That is not so. Rather, Isa, before leaving this earth, told His followers that they would receive

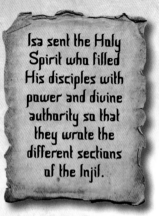

Isa sent the Holy Spirit who filled His disciples with power and divine authority so that they wrote the different sections of the Injil.

the Holy Spirit, God's Spirit, and that He would direct them to deliver His prophetic teachings to all mankind (see John 14:26).[13] So after Isa returned to heaven, He sent the Holy Spirit who filled His disciples with power and divine authority so that they wrote the different sections of the Injil. Again they did not do this on their own authority but with the authority of Isa and under the guidance of the Holy Spirit. This is clearly shown in the Injil:

❖ *Knowing this first of all, that no prophecy of Scripture comes from someone's own interpretation. For no prophecy was ever produced by the will of man, but men spoke from God as they were carried along by the Holy Spirit* (2 Peter 1:20-21).

---

[13] See also John 15:26, 16:11-13

As we can see, the prophets and apostles (followers of Isa) wrote God's words with the help and guidance of the Holy Spirit. So although men were involved in the writing of the Injil, the Bible is clearly God's book. Here is a brief description of its contents: The first 4 books of the Injil tell the life of Isa from four different perspectives. The fifth book, the Acts of the Apostles, tells the story of the early church and how Christianity spread. The next 21 books are letters written to instruct the early churches. The final book, Revelation, tells of Isa's second coming and kingdom.

New Testament Books						
History	Letters					Prophecy
Matthew	Paul's				General	Revelation
Mark	Early during missionary journeys	Later after arrest at Jerusalem			James	
Luke					Hebrews	
John	Galatians	First Imprisonment	Release	Second Imprisonment	Jude	
	1 Thess.				1 Peter	
	2 Thess.	Colossians	1 Timothy	2 Timothy	2 Peter	
	1 Cor.	Ephesians	Titus		1 John	
Acts	2 Cor.	Philemon			2 John	
	Romans	Philippians			3 John	

So then, what actually took place at the Council of Nicea? During this council in AD 325, the issue of Isa's essential nature and relationship to God the Father was discussed. Their special focus was on Arius, a false teacher who had led many believers astray by teaching that Isa did not fully share God's eternal nature. The end result of these meetings was that the 300 or so church leaders accepted the truth of Isa's divinity as taught in the Injil and then they wrote the 'Nicene Creed', a statement of faith which was then sent to churches in the Roman empire. Discussing the validity or genuineness of the Injil was not even a question on the table at the Council of Nicea. On the contrary, the church leaders present arrived at a common understanding regarding the nature of Isa by using verses from the same Injil, which they all possessed.[14]

In the early centuries of the church there were a number of church councils. However it must be noted that the church leaders did not gather to create or decide Christian theology but rather to clarify the teachings of the Injil. In fact, to think that these leaders would have wanted to destroy some Injils and put forward their own version makes no sense, because these were a group of devoted Christians, many of which suffered greatly for their faith. History tells us how committed they were to every detail of theology so that they spent weeks at Nicea making sure they affirmed the truth as portrayed in God's Word.

Wasn't the Original Injil the Injil of Barnabas?

There is another myth that many believe—that the original Injil was the Injil of Barnabas, which has remained hidden in the Vatican for centuries. From time

---

[14] Schaff, Philip, *History of the Christian Church* (Grand Rapids: Eerdmans, 1985) 3:330-365.

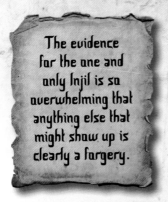

The evidence for the one and only Injil is so overwhelming that anything else that might show up is clearly a forgery.

to time we hear news of the "real" or "original" Injil being found somewhere in the Middle East. In fact one Muslim friend once asked me, if another "Injil" was found would you abandon your current Injil? I had to chuckle because he failed to understand that all the manuscripts of the Injil found to date are simply copies of the same original Injil which is in use all over the world today. In other words, the evidence for the one and only Injil is so overwhelming that anything else that might show up is clearly a forgery. The fact is that there is no other Injil, there has always been only one Injil which has been universally accepted by the followers of Isa and widely attested by thousands of ancient copies from the first century until today.

Regarding the famous Injil of Barnabas, the oldest manuscript of this book (composed of 222 chapters) is an Italian forgery and was written in the 15th century AD. By contrast the thousands of original manuscripts of the true Injil are in the Greek language and date very close to the time of Isa. Consequently it cannot be claimed that the Injil of Barnabas is genuine, because it was not written any time near to the time of Isa. Furthermore, during the early church age and up to the 15th century, there is no evidence that this Injil of Barnabas was ever used or recognized by the church.[15]

Injil of Barnabas

In fact, in terms of its content this "Injil" is filled with contradictions. The best example of this is that the author claims to have been a disciple of Isa. But among the 12 disciples of Isa no individual with the name of Barnabas ever appears. Even more important discrepancies come to surface. In the 20th chapter of the Injil of Barnabas, Isa is described as getting in a boat on the Sea of Galilee and going to Nazareth where he is met by sailors. But in fact the distance of 25 kilometers between these two places contains nothing but land and mountains. It would be like someone saying, "I traveled

---

[15] See: Geisler and Saleeb, 295-299

from Damascus to Beirut by boat." The author was clearly ignorant of Israel's geography.

Here is another error: According to the Injil of Barnabas (chapter 3, verse 217) Pontius Pilate was the Roman governor of Judea during the time of Isa's birth (4 BC) and his death (30 AD). But according to the Injil and other historical sources, Pilate was appointed as governor by Caesar Tiberius in 26 AD. In 1961 archeologists working on a dig in Caesarea, Israel, discovered a stone tablet with an inscription stating that Pilate was appointed governor during the time of Tiberius. If the writer of the Injil of Barnabas had truly been alive at the time of Isa he would not have made a mistake concerning Pilate's appointment as governor since Pilate was responsible for the death of Isa.

This book also contains important doctrinal errors: In the first chapters Isa is presented as the Messiah, but in later chapters (chapter 42, 97) it is stressed that Isa is *not* the Messiah. This shows that the Injil of Barnabas contradicts itself, the true Injil account, and also the Qur'an. Also, the Injil of Barnabas mentions nine levels in heaven (chapter 178), but this teaching corresponds only with Dante's 14th century *Divine Comedy*. Because of these and many other obvious errors and contradictions, theologians and historians have not taken this book's claims seriously.

So where did this fake "Injil" come from? From the bit of history available on this matter and even more from the content of this book, it is clear that it was written by someone who was trying to rewrite the true Injil in a way that would support the claims of Islam. So while the writer takes many portions from the true accounts of Isa, when it comes to His divine nature and His death on the cross, it denies these outright. He also adds in material that is foreign to the genuine Injil, namely, it adds prophecies of the coming of Muhammad. Clearly this author was trying to recreate the Injil in such a way that it would align itself with Islamic teaching.[16]

From time to time, claims of other "original" Injils surface, only to be discredited every time. There has only ever been one Injil—that which was accepted, protected, and used from the early Church age until now. We must also remember that Isa himself, the apostles, and leaders of the first church predicted that false teachers would rise up and spread lies and false teaching. For this reason it does not surprise us to find these types of false Injils because their appearance was predicted beforehand.

❖ *Beloved, do not believe every spirit, but test the spirits to see whether they are from God, for many false prophets have gone out into the world* (1 John 4:1).

To summarize, despite many attempts to create new Injils, our standard—the true Injil, God's original and unchangeable Word—has proven itself to be trustworthy down through the ages.

---

[16] See: Steer, 45-47.

So What About the Tawrat (Law) and Zabur (Prophets)?

In talking with my Muslim friends they often describe for me a sort of 'religious chronology' that they have heard since their childhood and which to them makes perfect sense. Perhaps you have heard this as well. It goes like this: "First God gave the Jewish people the Tawrat through the prophet Moses (Musa), but because of their disobedience and because the rabbis changed it, God then gave them the Zabur through the prophet David (Dawut). However with time the Zabur was also corrupted so God gave the Injil to the Christian community through Isa. Then after people tampered with the Injil and changed it, God finally decided to give the Qur'an to the Muslim community as a permanent and perfect book through the prophet Mohammed."

"Do not think that I have come to abolish the Law or the Prophets; I have not come to abolish them but to fulfill them."

When they tell me this story, I remind them that this story makes God appear as if He couldn't make up His mind, or that He had to keep changing His plan. They like to respond by pointing out that even human laws need to be changed from time to time. However, this is what I say, God is not a man and His thinking does not change or mature with time; His laws are eternal. The reality is that this type of story only makes God look like He does not know what He is doing. Not only that, but these claims also contradict God's specific promises to the contrary. Isa made it very clear that God's Word would never be corrupted or abolished.

❖ *Do not think that I have come to abolish the Law or the Prophets [Tawrat and Zabur]; I have not come to abolish them but to fulfill them. For truly, I say to you, until heaven and earth pass away, not an iota, not a dot, will pass from the Law until all is accomplished* (Matthew 5:17-18).

How logical would it be to believe in a God who can't make up His mind about His Word and has to keep changing His plan and send new books? Or suppose Isa, when He came, had said: "Don't worry about the Tawrat and Zabur. They are no longer necessary. My revelation is replacing all earlier holy books." Could you believe in Him if He said He was cancelling God's previous words and claiming to have the final say? I could not. It makes no sense for anyone sent from God to cancel what God has revealed before. As we read above, Isa clearly affirms the reliability of the Tawrat and Zabur.

God knows the future, so all of His words are, by necessity, perfect.

Furthermore, if God had actually given different people groups different revelations which invalidated previous ones, not only would He have created utter confusion in the minds of humans, but He would also be in serious contradiction with His own character. God is not a man who grows up and changes over time until he finally delivers a perfect revelation of Himself. God knows the future, so all of His words are, by necessity, perfect. And so we should expect God's Word to be one and the same, consistent with itself.

It is important to emphasize here the difference between cancelling and fulfilling. Isa made it very clear that He was not cancelling but fulfilling the words of the prophets. There is progression to the revelation of God as He slowly reveals more about Himself and His plan. There are also certain historical elements which unfold in the Bible. However when Isa al Masih arrived on the scene, we read that all of the promises made about Him met their fulfillment.[17] In this way Isa was the final piece of the puzzle.

Some point out that certain rituals spoken of in the Tawrat are no longer practiced by Christians today. For example, the Jews were instructed to kill a lamb as a sacrifice for their sins to God. And yet Christians today do not sacrifice animals. The reason for this is that those rituals described in the Tawrat were given as a reminder

---

[17] See: Matthew 1:22; 2:15; 4:14; 8:17; 12:17; 13:35; 21:4; 26:54-56.

Animal sacrifices were a reminder of how people's sins needed to be paid for with innocent blood.

of how people's sins needed to be paid for with innocent blood. And yet clearly an animal's blood cannot pay for the sins of a human.[18] Later in the Injil we find out that this was all a picture of how Isa al Masih would one day come as the Lamb of God to be sacrificed for the sins of the whole world. Thus because Isa *fulfilled* that picture and promise, we no longer need to shed the blood of animals.[19]

In summary, followers of Isa do not only accept the Injil as God's Word but they also accept God's previous revelations through the prophets, both the Tawrat and the Zabur. We call this "the Bible," which incorporates

---

[18] See: Hebrews 10:2-4.
[19] See: 1 Corinthians 5:7; Hebrews 10:11-12; 1 Peter 1:19.

all of God's Word and was given for the salvation of all mankind. In the Bible we find one message for all people of all time.

Isn't the God of the Old and the New Testaments Different?

This is a common question I am asked by my Muslim friends who have read portions of the Bible. Perhaps you are thinking this as well. "Is the God we see in the Old Testament different from God as revealed in the New Testament?" It is observed that in the Old Testament there are many references to God's law and His anger toward sin. However in the New Testament

All Christians believe that both the Old and New Testaments are God's Word.

God is described as loving, forgiving and merciful. Are they two different Gods or what? This is a common misunderstanding.

First let me clarify what Christians mean when they speak of the Old and New Testaments. All believers in Isa believe in both the Old and New Testaments. The Old Testament corresponds to the Tawrat and the Zabur, but it consists of more than just the writings of Musa and Dawut. Musa wrote the first five books of the Old Testament and Dawut penned most of the Psalms. However, aside from these, the Old Testament also includes God's revelation as written by several other prophets (Job, Solomon, Isaiah, Zechariah, and others). The Old Testament includes all of the prophets' writings before the time of Isa. These are a total of 39 separate books that were delivered to the people of Israel by God through the prophets.

The New Testament corresponds to the Injil but includes more than just the words of Isa. In it we find God's revelations to Isa's followers who wrote them down for the early believers. There are a total of 27 books in the New Testament. As we noted before, all Christians believe that both the Old and New Testaments are God's Word. Furthermore, we believe that these sacred writings all communicate the same message without canceling each other. In fact, we affirm with conviction that the words of the prophets from the beginning to the end point to the person of Isa. These were later fulfilled in the birth, death and resurrection of Isa al Masih as the Injil makes quite clear:

❖ *And He (Isa) said to them, O foolish ones, and slow of heart to believe all that the prophets have spoken! Was it not necessary that the Christ should suffer these things and enter into His glory? And beginning with Moses and all the Prophets, He interpreted to them in all the Scriptures [the Bible] the things concerning Himself* (Luke 24:25-27).

❖ *You search the Scriptures because you think that in them you have eternal life; and it is they that bear witness about Me* (John 5:39).

In this way the New Testament (Injil) is a fulfillment of the Bible's first half, the Old Testament (Tawrat, Zabur, and other books; see above). Both New and Old Testaments support each other, establishing a single revelation of God. In fact this is one of the most amazing miracles of God that the Bible, which is composed of a total of 66 different books, in spite of being written over a period of 1,500 years by 40 divinely inspired authors living in different places and times, actually maintains a unified structure and presents a consistent message.[20] Only God through His Spirit could have brought all these together into one book. That is why the Bible is called "the Word of God."

As with the Injil, there is abundant historical and archeological evidence that the writings of the Old Testament have been accurately preserved to this day. The best evidence of this is the Qumran scrolls found by a Muslim Bedouin shepherd near the Dead Sea in Israel. He found dozens of clay jars which contained hundreds of scrolls dating back to the time before Isa. In them ancient manuscripts of nearly every book of the Old Testament were found. Scholars who have examined these scrolls have found that they are in agreement with the modern Old Testament text we have today. Once again, we have historical and archeological information that confirms God's Word is unchanged and trustworthy.

---

[20] See: McDowell, 27-28.

The Qumran scrolls were discovered between 1946–1956 by a Muslim Bedouin shepherd near the Dead Sea.

However let us return to the question of why the God in the Old Testament seems different from the God described in the New Testament. This misunderstanding comes from failing to see the larger picture in God's plan. In the Old Testament after mankind rebelled against God, He was seeking to make Himself known to all nations. In order to do this He chose Abraham (Ibrahim) and made a covenant with His family. The nation of Israel, the direct descendants of Ibrahim, was to be an example to all nations. He taught them His laws. And yet because the Jews repeatedly failed God, He was forced to punish them. Soon it became evident that they would never be able to live according to His holy standard. This was an object lesson for all the nations of the world, namely, that man by his own efforts cannot please God. This is why God promised to send a Savior, Isa al Masih, to take all mankind's sin and punishment on the cross.

Throughout the Old Testament God promised to bring salvation and forgiveness through the promised Messiah. When we come to the New Testament, we find that God has kept His promise and that Isa was God's loving gift to mankind, a sacrifice to take away the sins of all people. In the Old Testament, God taught the Jews in particular (and all nations in general) that His Laws require people to live a perfect life and that the penalty for sin is death. But the Old Testament account shows that no one ever perfectly obeyed God and that this was not possible for humans. So in the New Testament, Isa al Masih came to bring salvation to all mankind. Thus it is clear that the Bible does not present two Gods but rather first shows us our imperfection in the light of God's Law; then in the New Testament shows us God's love in the perfect sacrifice of Isa.

Man by his own efforts cannot please God.

It is really a matter of perspective. We might at first assume that God has changed, but the reality is that our understanding of Him has grown with increased revelation. We could use the example of a child and his father. When a child is young he may think that his father is mean because he is always punishing him for his misbehavior. However as the child becomes a man he realizes that his father is not actually mean but that he loves him very much and that he only punished him to help him become a better man. In later years a son and his father may in fact become best of friends. So although the father was the same all along, it was the child's perspective that changed through maturity.

God's anger toward sin and His love for all people are shown throughout the entire Bible.

God and His character do not change. God's anger toward sin and His love for all people are shown throughout the entire Bible. The New Testament not only describes God's great love, but in the final book, Revelation, we find many terrifying descriptions of God's final judgment. Likewise, in the Old Testament, we have many examples of not only of God's wrath, but also of His great love for all people. One of the greatest examples is the life of Jonah (Yunus). Although he was a Jewish prophet, God called him to preach in the capital city of their enemies, in Nineveh of Assyria. Yunus was not interested and tried to run in the opposite direction. He did not want to warn the Ninevites of God's wrath or to offer them God's forgiveness. But he should have known that man cannot run from God. Soon he found himself caught in a great storm. Then he was thrown into the sea. God had mercy on him and soon a great fish swallowed him. Inside the belly of this creature, Yunus finally repented and agreed to go and preach to Nineveh. Through his preaching the whole city of Nineveh repented of their sin and turned to God who then forgave them and did not destroy their city. In the Old Testament, God clearly says, *"I have no pleasure in the death of the wicked, but that the wicked turn from his way and live"* (Ezekiel 33:11).

In summary, we see that God's Word is as trustworthy as God is—so why all the lies and misunderstandings about the Bible? Why do so many claim that it has been corrupted? Over time I have come to understand that

**God's preservation of Jonah illustrates
God's love for all nations.**

these claims are simply a way to keep people from reading God's Word. In fact I am convinced that Satan spreads these lies to keep people from searching for the truth about God. The only way to know for sure that the Bible is true, is to read it for ourselves. Sadly, most people who claim that the Injil has been changed have never even tried to read it. On the one hand they claim that the Injil is God's Word, but on the other hand they don't even make time to read it. And yet if the Injil is in fact God's message to us, then to not read it is to insult God. God's Word is truth and only it can set us free. Please read it for yourself!

> The only way to know for sure that the Bible is true, is to read it for ourselves.

Who Is Isa and
What Did He Do?

When my Muslim friends begin to read the Injil, they quickly come across another question. Throughout the Injil Isa is described as the "Son of God." This is blasphemous (*shirk*) to my Muslim friends because, in accordance with the Qur'an, they believe that God was not born and does not give birth. (The Qur'an specifically rejects the notion that Isa could be the "Son of God" see Al An'am 6:101; Al Jinn 72:3). So when the Injil states that Isa is the Son of God, Muslims assume that Christians must believe that God had sex with a woman to have a son. What my friends do not know is that I and all Christians fully agree

> All Christians fully agree with Muslims that God did not give birth to a son as a result of sexual union.

with them that God did not give birth to a son in this way. We all need to realize that when the Injil calls Isa the "Son of God," this does not refer to birth as a result of sexual union. The Injil tells us that God is spirit. A spirit cannot sleep with a woman to have a physical son. Rather, Isa is the *spiritual* Son of God in a very unique way that we will explain shortly.

There is another false claim that says that ancient Christians who did not know Isa personally wanted to make him into a god. In order to do this they came up with the idea that He was God's son. But this also is not true. Christ's followers did not invent the idea that He was the Son of God. The fact that Isa is the Son of God is clearly taught not only in the Injil but also long before in the Tawrat and Zabur.

It is easy for people to claim many things about Isa. Many of my Muslim friends are quick to tell me that they also believe in Isa and respect Him very much. I remind them that if they truly love Isa then they should at least read His book in order to find out the truth about Him. So, instead of paying attention to what others say, let us now look at what God's Word says about Isa.

The Testimony of the Prophets

Where does this idea that Isa would be the Son of God come from? First of all, we should emphasize that Christians believe in all the prophets as revealed in God's Word. The prophets who wrote God's words thousands of years before the Injil was written describe the coming of "the Messiah" (al Masih) in great detail. These include not just general or vague predictions about His coming but rather literally hundreds of clear prophecies regarding His person, birth, life, death, resurrection, and His future return to earth.[21] Here are just a few examples:

❖ *I will put enmity between you [Satan/Iblis] and the woman [Eve/Hawwa], and between your seed and her seed; He shall bruise your head, and you shall bruise His heel* (Genesis 3:15).

This is from the very first book of Musa which describes how Adam and Hawwa rebelled against God. Because of their sin, God had to punish them, but in doing so He also promised a Savior from the seed of the woman. From this verse we can see that one day a man described as "the seed of the woman" would crush the head of the serpent Iblis. This seems impossible because as we know the seed comes from the man not the woman. So who is this one who would finally defeat Satan? This is clearly describing Isa who was born of Mary (Maryam) while she was still unmarried and a virgin.

❖ *For dogs have surrounded Me; a band of evildoers has encompassed Me they pierced My hands and My feet. I can count all my bones. They look, they stare at Me; They divide My garments among them, and for My clothing they cast lots* (Psalm 22:16-18).

---

[21] See: Isaiah 7:14; Micah 5:2; Genesis 49:10; 2 Samuel 7:12; Isaiah 35:5-6; Zechariah 9:9; Isaiah 53; Psalm 16:10; Daniel 7:13-14.

These words were written by the prophet Dawut roughly 1000 years before the Injil. God had promised Dawut that the coming Savior would be from his family. In the Zabur, or Psalms, God often inspired Dawut to give descriptions of this great yet future Messiah. Here Dawut describes the Messiah suffering greatly. Not only that, but he says that His hands and feet are pierced. This is a clear description of how Isa was nailed to a cross. What is more amazing is the fact that death by crucifixion was unknown in the times of Dawut because it was only invented many centuries later by the Phoenicians. So it was impossible for him to know this. Later in the verse he describes how the soldiers who nailed Isa to the cross cast lots for His clothing. Ultimately everything described 1,000 years earlier by the prophet Dawut took place exactly as predicted.[22]

There are many more examples from the Tawrat and Zabur describing Isa which were written years before he was born. However, now let us focus on the verses that specifically describe His character. As mentioned earlier the fact that Isa would be called the "Son of God" was not something new in the Injil and was not invented by His followers. Long before Isa was born, the prophets had described Him as the coming Savior and Messiah. They further designated this promised King as the "Son of God." For instance, in the Old Testament God promised that one of King Dawut's descendants

---

[22] See: John 19:16-24.
[23] See: Carson, D.A. *Jesus the Son of God* (Crossway, 2012).

would establish the promised eternal kingdom. God tells Dawut that this great King who would come from his family would actually be the Son of God:

❖ *"He shall build for Me a house, and I will establish his throne forever. I will be his father and he shall be My son; and I will not take My lovingkindness away from him, as I took it from him who was before you. But I will settle him in My house and in My kingdom forever, and his throne shall be established forever"* (1 Chronicles 17:12-14).

Later in the Zabur Dawut writes about this great King and describes him again as the Son of God:

❖ *Serve the Lord with fear, and rejoice with trembling. Kiss the Son, lest He be angry, and you perish in the way, for His wrath is quickly kindled* (Psalm 2:11).

So we see that the promised Messiah, Isa, would be the Son of God, and that this was clearly predicted by the prophets in the Tawrat and Zabur.[23] However in order to answer the question of what it means for Him to be called the "Son of God" we need to turn to the Injil.

The Testimony of Gabriel (Jebril)

The Injil begins by telling us that Isa was from the family of Ibrahim and Dawut. This was important because Isa came as a fulfillment of the promises made to the prophets. Then we are introduced to Mary (Maryam) who is visited by the angel Gabriel (Jebril).

❖ *In the sixth month the angel Gabriel [Jebril] was sent from God to a city of Galilee named Nazareth, to a virgin betrothed to a man whose name was Joseph, of the house of David [Dawut]. And the virgin's name was Mary [Maryam]. And he came to her and said, "Greetings, O favored one, the Lord is with you!" But she was greatly troubled at the saying, and tried to discern what sort of greeting this might be. And the angel said to*

Mary visited by the angel Gabriel.

her, "Do not be afraid, Mary, for you have found favor with God. And behold, you will conceive in your womb and bear a son, and you shall call His name Jesus [Isa]. He will be great and will be called the Son of the Most High. And the Lord God will give to Him the throne of His father David, and He will reign over the house of Jacob forever, and of His kingdom there will be no end."

And Mary said to the angel, "How will this be, since I am a virgin?"

And the angel answered her, "The Holy Spirit will come upon you, and the power of the Most High will overshadow you; therefore the child to be born will be called holy—the Son of God" (Luke 1:26-35).

As you can see in this passage, the first one in the Injil to call Isa the "Son of the Most High (God)" is not a human being but the angel Jebril sent from God. The reason he gives for this is that Isa will be the great King promised to His ancestor Dawut. So clearly Isa is called the "Son of the Most High (God)" because of the prophecies that were given about Him in the Old Testament. Naturally this causes Maryam to become very confused because she is a virgin and had never slept with a man. Once again, Jebril stresses that Isa will not be the son of a man but rather the Son of God. This helps us to understand in what sense Isa is called the Son of God. Isa did not have a normal human father because of His miraculous birth; his only father was God Himself. That is why Isa always spoke of God as His Father. Again, this does not imply that God fathered him physically.

There are many instances in the Bible where the expression "son of . . ." is used in a non-literal meaning. The Jews liked to call themselves the "sons of Ibrahim." Clearly they were not fathered by the prophet Ibrahim. Isa went on to tell them that they were actually the sons of Satan. He did not mean that Satan had given birth to them but rather that they were acting like Satan.[24] In the same manner, when the Bible speaks of Isa as the Son of God, this has nothing to do with Him being physically or genetically related to God. On the contrary this is referring to a much higher level of relationship between God and Isa. Even in Arabic, people speak of a traveler as a "son of the road" (ibn al sabil) which clearly is a metaphoric expression. This reminds us that the word "son" (ibn) does not always include a physical relation.

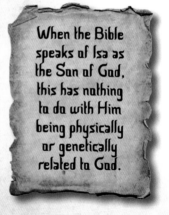

When the Bible speaks of Isa as the Son of God, this has nothing to do with Him being physically or genetically related to God.

---

[24] John 8:39-44.

The Testimony of God Himself

When Isa became a man, He began His public ministry by first being baptized by John the Baptist (Yahya). Yahya had been sent by God to prepare the way for the promised Messiah. He urged the Jewish people to repent of their sins and be washed symbolically in baptism.

Yahya told the crowds that soon the Messiah would arrive to establish God's Kingdom. Soon afterwards Isa al Masih came to Yahya. When Yahya saw Him he said: "*Behold the Lamb of God who takes away the sin of the world*" (John 1:29). He immediately recognized that Isa was the promised Savior.

When Isa was baptized, the Spirit of God descended on Him like a dove.

Isa then asked Yahya to baptize Him. While Yahya was baptizing Isa in the river, a most amazing thing happened.

❖ *And when Jesus [Isa] was baptized, immediately He went up from the water, and behold, the heavens were opened to Him, and He saw the Spirit of God descending like a dove and coming to rest on Him; and behold, a voice from heaven said, "This is My beloved Son, with whom I am well pleased"* (Matthew 3:16-17).

The voice from heaven is none other than the voice of God. Here clearly God was testifying to the fact that Isa was His beloved Son. This is important because many of my Muslim friends think that Christians have made Isa the Son of God. However, you can see from the verses quoted here that it is God Himself that called Isa His own beloved Son, and that the prophet Yahya was a witness to this event.

Shortly after Isa was baptized He began teaching and doing many miracles throughout the land. He healed the lame, gave sight to the blind, fed the hungry, and even raised the dead back to life. Not only that, but He also cast out the evil spirits that possessed people and set them free. He did so many miracles that they could not all be written down. However, He spent most of His time with His twelve disciples teaching them God's ways. One day He took three of His disciples with Him to a mountain and there they witnessed a most extraordinary event:

> ❖ *And after six days Jesus [Isa] took with Him Peter and James, and John his brother, and led them up a high mountain by themselves. And He was transfigured before them, and His face shone like the sun, and His clothes became white as light. And behold, there appeared to them Moses [Musa] and Elijah [Elias], talking with Him. And Peter said to Jesus, "Lord, it is good that we are here. If You wish, I will make three tents here, one for You and one for Moses and one for Elijah." He was still speaking when, behold, a bright cloud overshadowed them, and a voice from the cloud said, "This is My beloved Son, with whom I am well pleased; listen to Him"* (Mathew 17:1-5).

Again, the voice of God Himself is testifying to the truth that Isa is His beloved Son. But another important thing to note is that Peter first thought Isa was just a prophet like the other prophets Musa and Elias. He even offered to build a shelter for each of them. However very quickly the cloud covered them and God Himself corrects Peter by stating that Isa was not merely a prophet but rather the very Son of God. So clearly from God's perspective Isa was much more than a prophet— He was above them, He was the Son of God.

The Testimony of Isa Himself

As stated earlier, many think that early Christians tried to make Isa greater than He actually was. However it is important to see that in the Injil we read that Isa Himself confirmed His identity as the Son of God. After three years of serving people and healing their diseases, Isa was arrested by the Jewish leaders because they were jealous of His power and authority. They were also upset that He claimed to be the promised Messiah, the very Son of God. They had many false witnesses accuse Him, but were not successful because He was perfect in His life and character. Finally the Jewish leaders got to the real issue by asking Him who He was:

❖ *And the high priest (Jewish leader) stood up in the midst and asked Jesus [Isa], "Have You no answer to make? What is it that these men*

Even while judged, Isa declared that He is the Son of God.

testify against You?" But He remained silent and made no answer. Again the high priest asked Him, "Are You the Christ [al Masih], the Son of the Blessed One?" And Jesus said, "I am, and you will see the Son of Man seated at the right hand of Power, and coming with the clouds of heaven" (Mark 14:60-62).

Now if there was ever a good time for Isa to clear up any confusion about His identity this was His chance. If He was not the Son of God then He could simply say, "I am sorry you are mistaken, I have never claimed to be the Son of God." On the

This sonship is a special divine relationship between God and Isa al Masih.

contrary He affirms the truth that He is in fact the Son of God and further reminds those judging Him that one day He would return to earth to judge them. This made the Jewish leaders furious. They all said that Isa's claim to be God's Son was blasphemy (*shirk*), and they had Isa nailed to the cross because of this. So, in essence, Isa was put to death on a cross because of His statement that He was indeed the Son of God.

We have looked at the testimony of Jebril, Yahya, Isa al Masih, and God Himself that Isa is truly the Son of God. We have also seen that this sonship is not a physical or biological relationship but rather a special divine relationship between God and Isa al Masih. The Tawrat, Zabur, and Injil all say the same—that Isa is the Son of God. This is the clear teaching of God's Word:

> ❖ *And we have seen and testify that the Father has sent His Son to be the Savior of the world. Whoever confesses that Jesus [Isa] is the Son of God, God abides in him, and he in God* (1 John 4:14-15).

In fact, the Injil says that if we reject Isa as the Son of God, we are calling God a liar, because it is God Himself who has testified to the truth that Isa is His Son.

> ❖ *If we receive the testimony of men, the testimony of God is greater, for this is the testimony of God that He has given concerning His Son. Whoever believes in the Son of God has the testimony in himself. Whoever does not believe God has made Him a liar, because he has not believed in the testimony that God has given concerning His Son. And this is the testimony, that God gave us eternal life, and this life is in His Son. Whoever has the Son has life; whoever does not have the Son of God does not have life* (1 John 5:9-12).

Ultimately the question is this: Will we believe God's testimony or believe the opinions of others? If God says that He has a Son, then we must believe His Word. Is this somehow impossible for God? Clearly not! The Bible makes it clear that Isa is the Son of God. It also makes it clear that eternal life can only be obtained by believing in God's Son, Isa al Masih.

Did Isa Die on the Cross?

Another critical question regarding the life of Isa has to do with His death on the cross. My Muslim friends are often confused about this. Perhaps you also have been taught that Judas Iscariot, the disciple who betrayed Him, was made to resemble Isa and was thereby killed in His place. The story my Muslim friends often relate to me goes something like this: "When the Roman soldiers came to the garden of Gethsemane in the middle of the night to arrest Isa, they became confused and arrested Judas in Isa's place because God made Judas to resemble Him. They mistakenly arrested Judas and crucified him, while Isa was taken up into the presence of God without dying."

That is an interesting story, but it immediately raises questions:

> ➤ From a logical standpoint, is it not true that God performs miracles so that people might understand His work and come to know Him much better?

> ➤ If God secretly took Isa up to heaven while causing Judas to look like Isa and thus be killed, did He cause the people at that time to believe a lie?

> ➤ Could such a miracle match the righteous and holy character of God? Most assuredly not!

Likewise, if Judas was actually crucified in Isa's place, why would God wait 600 years until the birth of Islam to make this truth known? In that case God would have become the source of a false religion, Christianity, that had been spread all those years. In addition, tens of thousands of believers martyred for the cause of Isa would have gone to hell for believing in God's "miracle." If this were so then God would be acting deceitfully. For by the 6th century, the death and resurrection of Isa—a central teaching of Christianity—had become globally accepted, having been well documented by the Injil and by secular historians.

The truth as revealed in the Injil is that Judas did not die in Isa's place. Rather, after Judas had betrayed Isa, his conscience haunted him and he killed himself. Isa, on the other hand, after being unfairly tried, mocked, and severely beaten, was nailed to a cross upon which He died later the same day. His body was then placed in a cave that was used as a tomb. But that was not the end. Three days later God raised Isa al Masih from the dead. After appearing to his followers for 40 days, He returned to heaven to be with His Father.

In fact, in the weeks and months leading up to His death, Isa had repeatedly told His disciples that it was necessary for Him to die and be raised again.[25] Isa knew very well that His life's service would only be completed by His death and resurrection, because He himself said

---

[25] See: Matthew 16:21; 17:22-23; 20:17-18.
[26] Mark 10:45.

that He had come to give His life for mankind.[26] Not only that, but several hundred years before Isa was born the prophets had written that the promised Messiah would come to earth and die for the sins of the people. As an example, we can read what the prophet Isaiah wrote approximately 700 years before the birth of Isa:

❖ *Surely He has borne our griefs and carried our sorrows; yet we esteemed Him stricken, smitten by God, and afflicted. But He was pierced for our transgressions; He was crushed for our iniquities; upon Him was the chastisement that brought us peace, and with His wounds we are healed. All we like sheep have gone astray; we have turned—every*

Isa knew that His life's service would only be completed by His death and resurrection.

one—to his own way; and the Lord has laid on Him the iniquity of us all. He was oppressed, and He was afflicted, yet he opened not His mouth; like a lamb that is led to the slaughter, and like a sheep that before its shearers is silent, so He opened not His mouth (Isaiah 53:4-7).

It is impossible to find anyone else in history besides Isa who matches these predictions. Not only do the prophets tell of His death in great detail, they also speak of His resurrection from the dead. In the Zabur, the prophet Dawut speaks of Isa and says that His dead body would not decay.[27] A human corpse begins to decay on the third day but, amazingly, Isa rose from the dead on the third day. All of this and more was prophesied hundreds of years before Isa walked on this earth.

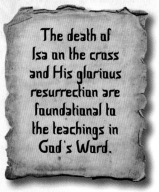

The death of Isa on the cross and His glorious resurrection are foundational to the teachings in God's Word.

When we look at the Injil, every book alludes directly or indirectly to Isa's death.[28] The death of Isa on the cross and His glorious resurrection are foundational to the teachings in God's Word. For this

---

[27] Psalm 16:10.
[28] See: Acts 2:23-32; Romans 5:6-8; 1 Corinthians 15:3-9; Hebrews 9:26-28; Revelation 1:18.

reason to deny that He died and rose from the dead is equivalent to denying the Word of God. It is because of Isa's resurrection from the dead that we have hope of one day being raised from the dead to eternal life in heaven with God.[29]

Historical records also verify that Isa was indeed crucified. For example, the Roman historian Tacitus (AD 56–120), who was not a Christian, mentions that Isa was crucified under the Roman governor Pilate.[30] During the second century AD the Greek historian Lucian mentions that the founder of Christianity had suffered the death penalty.[31] These and many other secular historians wrote about the life and death of Isa. In fact some of them criticized Christianity with bitter hatred. And yet none of them denied that Isa lived and died on the cross. The result is that, whichever historical source is consulted, throughout history the crucifixion of Isa has been accepted as an indisputable fact.

Furthermore, Isa's disciples who had been eyewitnesses of His death and resurrection spent the rest of their lives testifying to these facts. They risked their own lives for this truth, such that every one of Isa's disciples except for John was martyred on behalf of Isa. The central truth of the faith they proclaimed was the good news of His bodily resurrection after death. Clearly all of them would not die for something they knew

---

[29] See: 1 Corinthians 15:20.
[30] Geisler and Saleeb, 230.
[31] See: McDowell, 198.

was false. So the fact that they all sacrificed their lives for this truth only emphasizes their belief that Isa really died and physically returned to life.

So why exactly do my Muslim friends struggle accepting the truth of Christ's death and resurrection that is so clearly portrayed in the Tawrat, Zabur, Injil and in secular historical sources? Is it because the Qur'an, in the fourth surah An-Nisa verses 157-158, seems to imply that Isa did not die on the cross? However, it must be noted that other surahs speak of Isa as having died. In the third surah, Ali Imran verse 55, and in the fifth surah, Al Maidah verse 117, there is reference to Isa's death. Many Muslim scholars resolve this conflict by pointing out that in An-Nisa 4:157-158 it says that the Jews claimed to have killed Isa when in fact it was the Romans who did so. Whatever way Islamic scholars choose to resolve this issue, what is clear is that the death and resurrection of Isa are universally established facts.

The death and resurrection of Isa are universally established facts.

---

[32] See: Hebrews 11.
[33] See: Genesis 9:21; Exodus 2:12.
[34] Adam is called a "son of God" in Luke 3:38 because he had no earthly father besides God. However nowhere in the Bible is Adam called a prophet.

Why Did God Allow Isa to Die on the Cross?

This raises a more important question: Why did Christ die on the cross? Dear Muslim friend, perhaps you have difficulty accepting that God would permit Isa to die in such a horrible way. But remember death comes to all men. Even the greatest of the prophets died because they were humans. In fact many of them suffered greatly because of their faith in God.[32] So the fact that Isa died like so many before Him should not surprise us. However it is evident that His life and death are unique when compared to the other prophets, and so we must look deeper for our answer.

First we must clarify something with regard to the Bible's teaching on the prophets. Most Muslims believe that the prophets were sinless. But, the Tawrat and Zabur give us many examples of how even the prophets were not perfect.[33] By the grace of God they were honored to be messengers of God. And yet the Bible reminds us that they were *"men with a nature like ours"* (James 5:17). However Isa was very different because He never sinned. In fact even His enemies could find no fault with Him. Clearly Isa's death was not because of His own sins but rather, as Yahya said, He was a sacrifice for the sins of the whole world. It was Isa's willingness to lay down His life for all mankind that makes Him so unique and special.

Furthermore He was unique in His relationship to God. No other prophets were called the "Son of God."[34]

As we have seen from the testimony of God Himself, Isa al Masih was God's beloved Son. He was the promised Savior of the world.

No other prophets performed such a variety and volume of miracles. And even in His miracles Isa showed how different He was from the other prophets. On one occasion He was asked to heal a paralytic. Look at how Isa responded:

❖ *And when Jesus [Isa] saw their faith, He said to the paralytic, "Son, your sins are forgiven." Now some of the scribes were sitting there, questioning in their hearts, "Why does this man speak like that? He is blaspheming!*

Isa's miracles show how different He was from the other prophets.

Who can forgive sins but God alone?" And immediately Jesus, perceiving in His spirit that they thus questioned within themselves, said to them, "Why do you question these things in your hearts? Which is easier, to say to the paralytic, Your sins are forgiven, or to say, Rise, take up your bed and walk? But that you may know that the Son of Man has authority on earth to forgive sins"—He said to the paralytic—"I say to you, rise, pick up your bed, and go home." And he rose and immediately picked up his bed and went out before them all, so that they were all amazed and glorified God, saying, "We never saw anything like this!" (Mark 2:5-12).

The Jewish leaders were actually correct in saying that no human being could forgive the sins of men. But Isa al Masih was different. In order to prove to them that He had the divine right to forgive sins, He healed the man before their eyes. Clearly He was more than a mere human being. In fact Isa was more than a prophet.

Only Isa al Masih rose from the grave. Death could not keep him down.

In the end, Isa (like all the other prophets) died. However, only Isa al Masih rose from the grave. Death could not keep Him down. He crushed Satan and triumphed over death. He rose victorious to heaven where He is alive today. And we all, both Muslims and Christians, believe that in the Last Day it will be Isa who will return to this world. This should really make us think: If He was not merely another prophet, then who was He? Christians believe that He was in fact God's Word in human flesh. This leads us to the next question.

Do Christians Believe in Three Gods?

One of the most disturbing rumors about Christianity concerns the topic of the trinity or the 'three-in-one' doctrine. Many of my Muslim friends, and perhaps you as well, think that Christians worship three gods; that one of these gods is Mary (*Maryam*), and that we believe that she is God's wife.[35] This for them is *shirk*, a terrible blasphemy. As we have discussed, Christians do not believe that Isa was born as a result of God having physical relations with anyone. That is impossible and immoral. They also do not believe that Mary is a goddess or equal to God in any way. However we do believe in the Trinity based on interpretation of many Bible passages—but please allow me to explain it to you, then you can come to your own conclusions.

---

[35] This error was propagated by Mohammed's misunderstanding of true Christian teaching. See: Al Ma'idah 5:116.
[36] See: 1 Timothy 2:5.
[37] See: Mark 12:29.

The claim that Christians believe in three gods is simply not true. Not only does it contradict God's Word, but it also contradicts common sense. If God is perfect, then it is logically impossible to have another one like Him. Perfection demands oneness. If God is perfect in His character and complete in His attributes, then there can be no other God beside Him.

The Bible repeatedly states that there is only one God—He has no partners, associates, or rivals. The prophet Musa stated this very clearly when he said: "*The Lord our God, the Lord is One*" (Deuteronomy 6:4). Later the other prophets also emphasized this foundational truth:

❖ *Thus says the Lord . . . "I am the first and I am the last; besides Me there is no god"* (Isaiah 45:6).

God is infinitely greater than us — it is impossible for us to fully understand Him.

The Injil likewise testifies to the oneness of God's being.[36] Isa made it very clear that God is One.[37] However at this point we must be careful not to assume that because God is One He is therefore simple or easy to understand. God is infinitely greater than us and so we know that it is impossible for us to fully understand Him. Secondly we must remember that we can only fully know God by His revelation of Himself to us in His Holy Word. We must never forget that it is not our place to define who God is but rather we must allow Him to tell us who He is and how we should describe Him.

I believe that we too often try to simplify God. In emphasizing His oneness we can sometimes fall into the error of describing God as one-dimensional. However we must remember that He is much greater and more complex than even our greatest thoughts of Him. We all know that things are often much more complicated than they appear. This is most certainly the case with regard to God whom no man has seen. To help us understand this important point, let me use the human being as an example.

Human beings appear to the outside observer as a single being which we might call Ahmad or Aisha. However we also recognize that a human being is multi-dimensional. Humans are made up of many unseen elements—conscience, mind, soul and spirit—and yet these elements are all united in a single person. And yet, interestingly when a person dies and his spirit and/or soul depart from his body, this does not mean that he has become two or three beings. He is still considered to be a single being, for in the Last Day his spirit and/or soul will be reunited with his body.

So we see this concept of multiplicity in unity reflected even in our own beings. However, as we can see, believing in the multiple elements of our being does not deny our oneness. Likewise Christians affirm the oneness of God even as we believe in the Trinity as described in God's Word. The Trinity as shown in the Bible is that God is one being or essence and yet is made up of three persons called, the "Father," the "Son," and the "Holy Spirit." We see this taught in verses such as these:

❖ *Go therefore and make disciples of all nations, baptizing them in the name of the Father and of the Son and of the Holy Spirit* (Matthew 28:19).

❖ *The grace of the Lord Jesus Christ and the love of God and the fellowship of the Holy Spirit be with you all* (2 Corinthians 13:14).

In these verses we can clearly see that the Father, the Son, and the Holy Spirit are treated as equals—they are all represented as equals with God. Many of my Muslim friends naturally equate the Holy Spirit with the Ruhul Qudus of the Qur'an. However, it must be emphasized that the Holy Spirit mentioned in the Bible is God's Spirit, not an angel as some believe.

Again we must stress that the Trinity is not a concept that was made up by man. Had it been so, I'm sure we wouldn't have made it so difficult to understand. On the contrary this is the way God describes Himself, this is His self-revelation. It may be difficult for us to grasp this idea, but this does not mean that the concept itself is wrong, rather the problem is with the limited capacity of our human minds.[38] When we begin to believe we can comprehend God totally, we have set a trap for ourselves, for God is a being so great and majestic He exceeds human understanding. This is why we trust His Word and believe Him to be the God described in His Holy Word.

The Revelation of God in the Tawrat and Zabur

As we noted, the Bible does speak of God as consisting exclusively as one being. There is only one God. And while we hold firmly to this truth, we must also allow God to explain the inner workings of His being. Ultimately only He has the right to tell us what He is like, and the best place to learn this is in His revelation of Himself, the Bible. In His Word, we find that God often speaks of Himself using plural terms. In the very first chapter of the Tawrat, when God created Adam and Hawwa, He said: *"Let us make man in our own image."*[39] Notice that he uses "us" and "our," both plural forms. Furthermore, the name most often used for God in the Tawrat in the original Hebrew language is Elohim, which, interestingly, is a plural word. Then in the Zabur we come across some verses which clearly show a plurality in God's character:

❖ *Your throne, O God, is forever and ever. The scepter of Your kingdom is a scepter of uprightness; You have loved righteousness*

---

[38] Lewis, C.S. *Mere Christianity* (Harper Collins, 2001) 164-165.
[39] Genesis 1:26.

*and hated wickedness. Therefore God, your
God, has anointed You with the oil of gladness
beyond Your companions* (Psalm 45:6-7).

Here the prophet Dawut is speaking of God's final
reign. Then he suddenly speaks of God also anointing
God. The word "Messiah" means anointed one. God is
clearly anointing the promised Messiah (al Masih) who
is likewise designated as God.

❖ *The LORD says to my Lord: "Sit at My right
hand, until I make Your enemies Your
footstool"* (Psalm 110:1).

Again we find the Lord God speaking to another
who He also calls Lord telling Him to sit at His right
hand, clearly a position of privilege. Later, when Isa al
Masih is risen from the dead, the Injil says that *"He
sat down at the right hand of the Majesty on high"*
(Hebrews 1:3). All this may be confusing at first but
it simply serves to remind us that both the Tawrat
and Zabur speak of God in plural form. So the Old
Testament testifies to both the Oneness and Plurality
of God's nature. Only when we come to the Injil do we
learn how these actually fit together.

The Revelation of God in the Injil

When we come to the Injil we find that Isa is the
fulfillment of all the promises regarding the Messiah
in the Old Testament. Clearly no mere human being or
prophet could teach with such authority or do the signs
and wonders that Isa did. And yet as we saw earlier, the

fact that He was called the Son of God made the Jewish leaders very angry because they did not believe in Him. They thought He was blaspheming. But in reality He was the promised Messiah, the very Son of God.

In the Injil, the first verses in the book of John give a clear description of who Isa really was:

❖ *In the beginning was the Word, and the Word was with God, and the Word was God. He was in the beginning with God. All things were made through Him, and apart from Him nothing came into being that has come into being* (John 1:1-3).

We read here about the "Word of God" (Kalamullah), a name that also appears in the Qur'an with reference to Isa.[40] The above text says clearly that God's Word has always existed with God. It was this Word of God that created the whole universe when God commanded everything to exist. God's Word is clearly His honor and glory. However a few verses later in the same chapter, we read something amazing about this Word:

❖ *And the Word became flesh and dwelt among us, and we have seen His glory, glory as of the only Son from the Father, full of grace and truth* (John 1:14).

The Injil clearly tells us that God's eternal Word, the same Word who created the whole universe actually

---

[40] An Nisa 4:171.

became human and lived on this earth. We are told that this Word was in fact the glorious Son of God. What does this mean? Clearly one's word is a representation of one's character. The person described as the Word of God here (Kalamullah) is a physical representation or revelation of God's holy character. In short, Isa was God's Word in human form.

Do you struggle to understand this? I don't blame you if you do. It is hard to grasp. How could a man be God? First, we must remember that God can do anything He wishes. Also it is helpful to remember that according to the Bible a man did not become God, but rather God *chose* to become a man. So this action was initiated by God who is able to do as He pleases. No one can tell God what He can or cannot do. He is free to do as He pleases.

> Man did not become God, but rather God chose to become a man.

Secondly, this is not the only example in the Bible of God taking a physical form in order to communicate to mankind. You will be familiar with the story of God appearing to Musa in a burning bush (see Exodus chapter 3). When Musa was still a shepherd, God appeared to him in a bush that was burning but amazingly was not consumed by the flames. The Bible says that God's glorious presence was in the bush and that through it He spoke to Moses in a visible way. None of us have a

God spoke to Moses through the burning bush.

problem believing that God could or would use a simple bush to show His glory to man. And yet we somehow struggle believing that God would use a human body to show Himself to us. The fact is that God's glorious Word took flesh in Isa al Masih and showed His light to all mankind.

The real question is not if God did this, but why He did this? Up until the time of Isa, God had sent many prophets to teach His people how to live. And yet, mankind rejected His words and lived in rebellion. Even though God repeatedly warned them of punishment, it became clear that human beings would never be reformed on their own. Sending prophets was not enough, because mankind needed a change of heart, not just more laws. So finally God Himself intervened to save mankind. Isa al Masih was God's revelation of Himself in human flesh. Isa, after living a perfect life, sacrificed Himself for all mankind on the cross. This was the final and complete solution to man's sin and rebellion. But, because Isa was perfect, He did not stay in the grave. Three days later He arose victorious over sin and Satan. Isa is alive in the presence of God, seated at His right hand. He is also the one who will soon return to save all who have believed in Him and to judge

God Himself intervened to save mankind.

His enemies in the Last Day. All this and more is what makes Isa so unique and special. This is why Christians believe that He alone can save us.

What Is the Relationship Between Christianity and Islam?

Many of my Muslim friends and other people that I meet claim to believe in Isa and enjoy hearing about Him. Unfortunately, although most claim to believe in Isa and the Injil very few actually take the time to read the Injil for themselves. One reason is because they think the Qur'an has replaced the Injil as God's final revelation. They believe that the Qur'an encompasses all the teachings of the Bible. This is easy for them to say when they have not read the Qur'an and the Bible or compared them for themselves.

You may want to ask me, "Have you read the Qur'an?"—Yes I have! Another question you may want to ask is "What do you think about Muhammad?" I always try to answer in a respectful and sensitive manner. We have different religious views, and are free to have our own opinions. However we should all be careful to respect the religious values of others. So, as I respond to your questions regarding Islam in this chapter, please remember that I love and respect all Muslims and that my desire is not to offend anyone but to show the truth as it is revealed in God's Word.

Does the Injil Predict
the Coming of Muhammad?

My Muslim friends, often say something like "we accept all of the prophets and consider Isa as an especially important prophet. So why do you not accept our prophet?" Often an additional claim is made—"Several verses in the Injil predict the coming of Muhammad." The way this is explained is to use the Greek word '*parakletos*' found in the Injil, whom Isa said would come after Him. It is said that, the Greek word '*parakletos*', translated 'helper' which appears in the book of John,[41] was actually '*periclutos*' which means "praised one" in the original Injil in Greek. One of Muhammad's titles is "Ahmad" in surah As Saf 61:6. "Ahmad" in Arabic means "praised one," so it seems equivalent to the Greek term '*periculos*'. Thus Muslims believe that Isa spoke of the coming '*periculos*' instead of '*parakletos*' and that He was in fact predicting the coming of Muhammad after Him.

First of all we must note that in thousands of manuscripts of the Injil not one of them has the word '*periclutos*'.[42] Furthermore, the original meaning and object of this word '*parakletos*' is very clear within the text itself. This Greek word actually describes one who comes alongside to help, support, or comfort another. The context in which this word is used is of

---

[41] See John 14:16-17, 26: 15:26; 16:7, 13-14.
[42] See: Geisler and Saleeb, 153.
[43] John 14:17

utmost importance. When Jesus spoke of this 'helper,' He specifically explained who he was and what he would do. When we read the verses with reference to the *parakletos* the functions of the promised helper are obvious:

- ❖ *He will be with you forever* (John 14:16).

- ❖ *The world does not accept Him, does not see or know Him* (John 14:17).

- ❖ *He is living among you and will be in you all* (John 14:17).

- ❖ *The Father will send Him in My name* (John 14:26).

- ❖ *He will remind you of My words* (John 14:26).

- ❖ *He will testify of Me (Isa)* (John 15:26).

- ❖ *When He comes He will convince the world of sin, righteousness and judgment* (John 16:8).

- ❖ *He will lead you into all truth* (John 16:13).

- ❖ *He will not speak from Himself, He will make known what will take place* (John 16:13).

- ❖ *He will glorify Me (Isa) and reveal My words to you* (John 16:14).

When we consider all the verses listed here, we realize that Isa was not talking about any normal human being. These could only be attributed to the Holy Spirit as described in the Bible. In fact, Jesus made it clear who He had in mind when He specifically called the *parakletos* the *"Spirit of truth."*[43] Thus it is not possible for Muhammad or any other human to fill this role, for the *parakletos'* characteristics listed above go beyond any normal human being. Not to mention the fact that the Holy Spirit already existed at that time and was soon to live inside the disciples.

When we read further in the Injil, we come to the first chapters of Acts, the book immediately following the book of John. There we see the fulfillment of the promises Isa made concerning the *parakletos* which took place ten days after Isa was taken up into heaven. On the day of Pentecost, at the birth of the Church, we read how the Holy Spirit descended upon the believers with awesome power. So, just as Isa promised in John 14:17, the Holy Spirit began to live inside every one of His followers and continues to do so to this day.

At Pentecost, the Holy Spirit decended upon believers with awesome power.

The truth is that it runs contrary to the teaching of the Injil for another prophet to come after Isa. For as the prophets had made known beforehand, God provided a perfect salvation for all men through Isa by means of His death and resurrection. Therefore, for God to send a new revelation or a new way of faith through yet another prophet would create a contradiction and thereby invalidate the message of Isa. In fact, in the final book of the Injil, Isa Himself specifically states that no further revelation will come and no one can add or subtract from God's Word.

> ❖ *I warn everyone who hears the words of the prophecy of this book: if anyone adds to them, God will add to him the plagues described in this book, and if anyone takes away from the words of the book of this prophecy, God will take away his share in the tree of life and in the holy city, which are described in this book* (Revelation 22:18-19).

In summary, we can say that the Injil does not say a single word about the coming of another prophet after Isa. If the Injil had in fact predicted the coming of Muhammad, then we Christians would have been the first to know of it and believe in him because we are not unbelievers but are rather "People of the Book" (Ahl al Kitab) who believe in all of God's revelation. Likewise, if God had wanted to announce that another prophet would came after Isa, He would not have limited himself to one or two verses in the Injil which provide no clear picture. Rather, as we see in the Old Testament regarding the coming of Isa, we would expect Him to have announced Muhammad's coming in numerous books in the Injil and to have given many clear and supernatural indicators to enable believers to recognize and accept him. So it is not the Christian's choice to accept or not accept Muhammad as a prophet; on the contrary it is Isa and the Injil that leave no room for another prophet.

Why Don't Christians Accept the Qur'an as a Holy Book?

Another frequent question I encounter from my Muslim friends is, "We accept your book; why don't you accept our book?" I respond by saying, "Let me ask you a question. What do you mean by 'accepting a book?'" To me it means understanding and believing the content of a book and living accordingly. Consequently, to my friends who claim to accept the Injil, my response is, "Do you believe that Isa is the Son of God, and that He died for the sins of the world? Because that is the Isa of the Bible." If their answer is, "No! We only accept him as a prophet," it means that those who say "we accept your book" are in fact rejecting the essential message of the Injil.

While we should respect each other's religious values, this does not mean that we must accept each other's religion.

Another thing my readers should note is that while we should *respect* each other's religious values, this does not mean that we must *accept* each other's religion. It is also a fact that Muhammad was not the last prophet to claim that God sent him after Isa as God's final revelation or prophet. Many people are not aware that many other men have claimed to be prophets since the time of Muhammad. Does that mean that Muslims or indeed any of us must accept these newer prophets? For example, in the 19th Century in Iran, one named

Everything was fulfilled in Isa, so that all who believe in Him are forgiven all their sins.

Baha'u'llah claimed to be a prophet and he established the religion known as Baha'i. He taught that he was the final prophet in line with Musa, Isa, and Muhammad. So because he claimed these things do we need to accept him too? Of course not!

According to God's revelation proclaimed in the Old and New Testaments, everything was fulfilled in Isa, so that all who believe in Him are forgiven all their sins.[44] Consequently, to add any other supplemental revelation to His Word would mean that His previously finished revelation is lacking or invalid. And for God to declare His own word invalid goes totally against His

---

[44] See: John 3:16-18; Acts 4:12; Romans 3:21-31.

character and attributes because God cannot change or lie. Secondly, the Injil repeatedly emphasizes that after its completion there would be no more written revelation from God. In the last book of the Injil, we have the section called 'Revelation' where Isa appears and is called *"the First and the Last, the Beginning and the End"* (Revelation 22:13). Clearly the Injil teaches that Isa was the final revelation of God.

As explained before, the Injil is the continuation and completion of the Tawrat and Zabur. All these in fact form one book called the Bible. Most of my Muslim friends think that the Injil came to replace the Tawrat or Zabur. Actually, the Injil is like the puzzle piece that perfectly completes the Tawrat and Zabur. The Zabur closes with the promise and expectation of the Messiah Isa.[45] Clearly the Old Testament by itself is an unfinished book. However with the coming of Isa in the Injil God has placed the final piece into the puzzle of His plan and so at the end of the Injil it is clear that no other prophet will come. Notice what the Injil says on this matter.

❖ *Long ago, at many times and in many ways, God spoke to our fathers by the prophets, but in these last days He has spoken to us by His Son, whom He appointed the heir of all things, through whom also He created the world. He is the radiance of the glory of God and the*

---

[45] See: Malachi 3-4.
[46] At Tawbah 9:30; Maryam 19:8-92.

exact imprint of His nature, and He upholds the universe by the word of His power. After making purification for sins, He sat down at the right hand of the Majesty on high, having become as much superior to angels as the name He has inherited is more excellent than theirs. (Hebrews 1:1-4).

It is true that the Qur'an retells or at least alludes to many of the stories found in the Old and New Testaments. However it clearly denies the foundational truths of Christianity. People who have thoroughly compared the holy books note that there are many similarities (which we would expect, as there are common and shared moral teachings among most religions). However, these scholars also note that there are essential differences. In particular, when it comes to the person and work of Isa, the Qur'an deviates completely from the truths spoken by God in the Injil, and the Qur'an even manifests discrepancies within itself on this all-important subject.[46]

As seen earlier, the Tawrat, Zabur, and Injil all agree that Isa is the Son of God, that He came into the world to save sinful humans through His death and resurrection, and that salvation cannot be attained by human works but only through faith in Isa. But the Qur'an does not accept these three critical truths which are the foundation of the Bible. And yet the Injil itself states, if Isa did not die and rise from the dead, our faith and hope are in vain (see 1 Corinthians 15:17-19). For this reason we cannot deny these foundational teachings, or we will have denied the very truth of God as revealed in the Bible.

The truth is, God's revelation has never changed. God is one and His revelation is one. It started in the Tawrat with God's law and continued in the Zabur in which God's prophets spoke of a coming Messiah. Then in the Injil, Isa proved to be the fulfillment of those promises and through His death and resurrection provided a way of salvation for all mankind. So we see that all three books actually form one book because together they present God's complete message of salvation. Unfortunately the same cannot be said regarding the Qur'an. Although it appears to agree with the Bible on some points, when it comes to the foundational issues it takes a different path and proclaims a different message to that of the Tawrat, Zabur, and Injil.

At this point, dear Muslim friend, you might ask me to elaborate on the differences that I have found between the Qur'an and the Bible. I am concerned that I might offend you. To use an example: suppose I visited a friend's hometown and I began to compare my city with his city; he would likely take offense. This is because he has not seen my home and cannot understand the comparisons I make. So instead of comparing them I would prefer to invite him to visit my hometown so he can see the differences for himself. In the same way, instead of telling the differences that I have found between the Qur'an and the Bible, I invite you to read it for yourselves. Otherwise when I give my conclusions you might be confused and think that I am insulting your religion. What each of us believe about the Qur'an and the Bible is such an important matter that each of us needs to research the sources ourselves instead of simply listening to other's opinions.

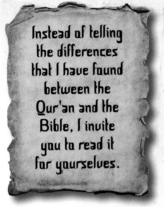

Instead of telling the differences that I have found between the Qur'an and the Bible, I invite you to read it for yourselves.

This reminds me of a time I had a discussion with an Imam. He was very angry that I was offering my books to people who wanted to read them. After going on for a good while about how we were "brainwashing" people, he finally let me respond. I told him that in one way we are very similar to each other but in another way very different from one other. We are similar in that we are both very devoted to our faith and passionate about our beliefs. However, then I asked him what he knew about God's Word. He told me that he had memorized much of the Qur'an. I congratulated him but then I asked him if he had also read the Tawrat, Zabur, and Injil. He said he didn't need to do so. To this I responded that this was the essential difference between us. I have read the Tawrat, Zabur, and Injil, as well as the Qur'an and many other religious books. After reading them all and comparing them to one another, I have come to possess full confidence that the Bible alone is God's Word. So while his decision was based on only one option, my decision is based on comparing as many options as possible.

I often tell my friends that this is like saying, "My city is the most beautiful city in the world!" Now if you have traveled most of the world and can compare your city with others then you have a right to declare this. But if you have never been out of your city how can

We must be willing to ask the hard questions about what we have been taught.

you say such a thing? We cannot assume that what we have been taught is the only truth. This may be very difficult for us but we must be willing to ask the hard questions about what we have been taught.

As I said at the outset, the fact that we don't see eye to eye on all these issues doesn't make us enemies. Rather, I love my Muslim friends and enjoy discussing these important matters with them. In fact I often urge them to read not only the Injil but also the Qur'an so they can compare the books for themselves and make a better decision about what to believe. The fact, that God's revelation starting with the Tawrat, throughout the Zabur, and up through the Injil is entirely consistent, is nothing less than a miracle. However I challenge my Muslim friends to ask "Why is the Qur'an not in line with God's revelation in the Bible?" It is an important question for each one of us to research for himself.

Why Are Christians
at War with Islam?

As is the case in much of the world, my Muslim friends like to talk politics. I am often asked why America does this or that. When I say I don't know, they are surprised. They assume that if I am a Christian then I must be involved in politics, so they are disappointed to find out that I don't represent any political view. This misconception comes from wrongly associating Christianity with Western powers. When Western countries are involved in any war in the Middle East they assume that Christians are warring with Muslims again.

This notion, unfortunately, has a long and sad history leading all the way back to the Crusades of the Middle Ages. At that time popes and European kings organized a series of armed campaigns to take back Jerusalem and other holy sites from the Muslims. What most Muslims don't know is that we Christians condemn the bloodshed and misery caused by these Crusades just as much as they do. Naturally they are confused because they think that if the Crusades were begun by Christians, how is it that Christians today can condemn them? In order to untangle this problem we must look back to the Word of God.

Ever since Cain (Qabil) and Abel (Habil), people have been fighting over anything and everything. This is a sad result of Adam's sin as it was passed on from generation to generation. Nations have often fought with their neighbors, conquering lands, and forming empires. Many wars have even been fought in the name of religion. The real question is, does God want us to fight for Him? Isa answered this question in a most amazing way. Look at what He said:

❖ *You have heard that it was said, "You shall love your neighbor and hate your enemy." But I say to you, Love your enemies and pray for those who persecute you, so that you may be sons of your Father who is in heaven. For He makes His sun rise on the evil and on the good, and sends rain on the just and on the unjust. For if you love those who love you, what reward do you have? Do not even the tax collectors do the same? And if you greet only your brothers, what more are you doing than others? Do not even the Gentiles (Kafir/Infidels) do the same? You therefore must be perfect, as your heavenly Father is perect* (Matthew 5:43-48).

> Isa taught that through love we could even make friends of our enemies.

Isa clearly commanded us not to seek revenge. In fact He taught that through love we could even make friends of our enemies. Later on, when Isa was being arrested by the Jewish leaders, one of His disciples,

Peter, tried to intervene by attacking them with his sword. Isa immediately stopped him saying, *"All who take the sword will perish by the sword"* (Matthew 26:52). Again, clearly Isa did not allow His followers to war for His cause.

So while the teaching of Isa is clear on this subject, people are sometimes confused by other words of Isa. For example Isa said, *"Do not think that I have come to bring peace to the earth. I have not come to bring peace, but a sword"* (Matthew 10:34). In this instance it appears as if Isa is contradicting His earlier teaching. However when we read the rest of that passage we find that He is in fact not talking about His followers taking the sword and attacking others, but rather that Christians will suffer greatly by the sword. He even tells His followers that their own family members would try to kill them.

When we look at the spread of Christianity we find that the followers of Isa did not spread their faith by fighting or invading countries. Rather they were constantly hunted and killed for their allegiance to Isa and their belief in his death and resurrection. Many of Isa's early followers were thrown to the wild beasts as food to entertain crowds of people in Roman stadiums. And yet these Christians never sought revenge because the Injil taught them not to seek revenge but to leave the final judgment with God.[47]

---

[47] See Romans 12:19-21

For the first 300 years, the Christians multiplied despite much suffering. Afterwards the Roman Emperor Constantine became a Christian and made it much easier for them. However after the Roman State adopted Christianity as its official religion, they soon began to use it to control the people. Over time the Roman "Church" strayed further and further from Isa's teaching, began killing pagans, and even persecuted Christians who remained faithful to the teachings of Isa. During this period, the State "Church" began to be governed by the pope who became like an emperor. Centuries later it was one of these popes who ordered the first Crusade. So the Crusades of the Middle Ages in fact don't represent the teaching of Isa or the beliefs of true Christians at all.

Unfortunately many of my Muslim friends assume that the Pope or Western powers represent Christianity. Please remember that Isa is the founder of our faith and

Christians were killed for their faith in Isa.

> **The Crusades of the Middle Ages don't represent the teaching of Isa or the beliefs of true Christians.**

that only His teachings represent the truth. Popes or other church leaders are only human beings who may or may not represent the true teachings of Isa. I ask you not to judge Isa or His followers by what you watch on the evening news or what you read in your history books, but to read the Injil instead to find out what Isa al Masih really taught. True Christians, according to Isa, are not those who just call themselves believers but rather those who actually follow His commands.[48] Ultimately, Isa is our model and leader.

> **Church leaders are human beings who may or may not represent the true teachings of Isa.**

❖ *For to this you have been called, because Christ also suffered for you, leaving you an example, so that you might follow in His steps. He committed no sin, neither was deceit found in His mouth. When He was reviled, He did not revile in return; when He suffered, He did not threaten, but continued entrusting Himself to Him who*

---

[48] John 14:15

judges justly. He himself bore our sins in His body on the tree, that we might die to sin and live to righteousness. By His wounds you have been healed. For you were straying like sheep, but have now returned to the Shepherd and Overseer of your souls (1 Peter 2:21-25).

It is true that there are many who call themselves Christians, and yet *do not actually* follow in Isa's steps. This problem exists in all religions. I have met many people who call themselves Muslims, and yet their behavior and life-style clearly contradict what is written in the Qur'an. However, it is important not to judge a religion only by its followers; more importantly we must consider its founder's life and teachings. In seeking to understand the true difference between Christianity and Islam, it doesn't necessarily help to look at modern-day people who call themselves "Muslims" or "Christians." We need to compare the teachings and life of Isa with that of Muhammad. Which one's life is the best example of God's perfect character and love for mankind? Which of them can I follow with confidence? Answering this question is essential to understanding the truth of God.

For us who truly seek to follow Isa, we are commanded to love all people, including our Muslim friends, with the love the Isa showed us on the cross. In fact, even as He was being nailed to the cross, Isa said, *"Father forgive them for they know not what they do"* (Luke 23:34). This forgiving and loving spirit is the essence of true Christianity.

What Are Christian Beliefs and Practices

For most of my Muslim friends, when they hear the word "Christian," it brings to mind many conflicting ideas. This is why *I prefer to call myself a follower of Isa.* All too often the word "Christian" is associated with things seen on TV. And yet, simply because an actor wears a necklace with a cross, or a politician goes to church on Sunday doesn't make them a follower of Isa. Naturally it is hard for people to distinguish between what is truly the teaching of Isa and what is simply Western tradition or Hollywood fiction. Because of this, it is important to look at the Injil and find out for ourselves what Isa actually taught.

Most of my Muslim friends in the Middle East haven't had the opportunity to meet many Christians, and thus are curious to know what they believe and how they live. A lot of their ideas about Christianity have been picked up from the media, and they rarely reflect what the Injil teaches. In fact many of these ideas regarding Christianity are grossly mistaken and misinterpreted. In the following paragraphs I hope to clear up these misconceptions by looking at God's Word.

Are Christians Free to Live Immorally?

Sadly many of my Muslim friends believe that Christians are free to live immoral lives. It is thought that Christians have no morals and are free to commit as many sins as they like so long as they confess to a priest on Sunday. Again, the reason for this is the assumption that what they see on Western television is representative of true Christianity. Nothing could be further from the truth.

Let's look again at the idea that we can confess our sin to the priest and that he can somehow grant us forgiveness. You may be surprised to find out that many of us don't believe in or follow that practice.

The Injil makes it very clear that only God can forgive sins.

The Injil makes it very clear that only God can forgive sins.[49] It also says that God will judge us for our sins. So where does the priest get the right to forgive sins? Here again we have a misunderstanding because priests do not claim to have the right to forgive anyone's sins but rather they listen to people's confessions and urge them to repent before God and seek His forgiveness. On this basis, priests may assure repentant people from God's own Word that God has forgiven their sins.[50]

---

[49] 1 Timothy 2:5
[50] See: 1 John 1:9, James 5:14-16, Ephesians 4:32.

About living immorally, most of my Muslim friends are shocked to find the high moral standard set by Isa on this subject. Look for example at what He said regarding adultery:

> ❖ *You have heard that it was said, "You shall not commit adultery." But I say to you that everyone who looks at a woman with lustful intent has already committed adultery with her in her heart. If your right eye causes you to sin, tear it out and throw it away. For it is better that you lose one of your members than that your whole body be thrown into hell* (Matthew 5:27-29).

Clearly Isa did not allow for even a hint of immorality. In fact Isa made it quite clear that even looking at a woman with lust in our hearts is equal to adultery.

Isa did not allow for even a hint of immorality.

Later in the same chapter, Isa touches on the subject of marriage and makes it very clear that divorce is not God's will. The Injil stresses the holiness of marriage as a union of one man with one woman that should last for life. This is the case because both men and women were created equal in God's image. Unfortunately, immorality in most Western countries is going from bad to worse, with divorce rates sky-rocketing and sexual immorality out of control. And yet regarding this subject the Injil is clear:

❖ *But sexual immorality and all impurity or covetousness must not even be named among you, as is proper among saints. Let there be no filthiness nor foolish talk nor crude joking, which are out of place, but instead let there be thanksgiving. For you may be sure of this, that everyone who is sexually immoral or impure, or who is covetous (that is, an idolater), has no inheritance in the kingdom of Christ and God* (Ephesians 5:3-5).

True followers of Isa should have a desire to live a holy life full of love for all mankind.

It is true that Isa gave us freedom, but this is freedom from sin, not freedom to sin as much as we like. True followers of Isa should have a desire to live a holy life full of love for all mankind as He did.

Another reason for this misconception is that when I tell my Muslim friends that we are forgiven of our sins by simply believing in Isa they then say to me: "Well if salvation is that easy, then after believing you can go on sinning as much you like." Of course this reaction would be totally wrong. In fact the Injil also counters this notion by saying, *"How can we who died to sin still live in it?"* (Romans 6:2). The whole reason true Christians believe in Isa is to be free from the power of sin in our lives, so it makes no sense for us to continue as slaves to sin. This does not mean that we become perfect or stop sinning entirely. Rather, it means that we regularly repent and seek God's forgiveness when we sin and work hard to live a life honoring to God:

> **We regularly repent and seek God's forgiveness when we sin and work hard to live a life honoring to God.**

❖ *This is the message we have heard from him and proclaim to you, that God is light, and in Him is no darkness at all. If we say we have fellowship with Him while we walk in darkness, we lie and do not practice the truth. But if we walk in the light, as He is in the light, we have fellowship with one another, and the blood of Jesus His Son cleanses us from all sin. If we say we have no sin, we deceive ourselves, and the truth is not in us. If we confess our sins, He is faithful and just to forgive us our sins and to cleanse us from all unrighteousness* (1 John 1:5-9).

The Bible clearly commands us to live lives that are in accordance with God's holy standards. When we sin, we must immediately confess and repent of that sin. So for those that think being a Christian is easy (because they don't have to worry about their sin), the Injil makes it clear that if we follow Isa we must seek to live perfect lives like He did.

Which Church Is True Christianity?

Another thing that confuses my Muslim friends is the large variety of Christian churches and denominations, especially in the West. They ask me, "Which of these is the right church?" While it may seem confusing at first, really all we need to do is go back to the source. During Isa's life on earth, He said the following about the Church: *"I will build my church, and the gates of hell will not prevail against it"* (Matthew 16:18). Isa clearly promised to establish His own church. He further promised that nothing could ever destroy it. Clearly He is not speaking of a particular building or structure, but rather of all those who follow Him.

> The true church of Isa is the univeral assembly of believers who have held faithfully to His teachings from the beginning.

Needless to say, when we look at churches today, we can't help but see that instead of the one church Isa had in mind, there are various denominations all very different from one another, especially in matters of religious practice. My friends often ask: "Don't they all use the same Injil?" Of course, they do. Yet the reality is that for the last 2,000 years since Isa walked on this earth, many different teachers have come with different interpretations of the Injil, and many different kinds of churches have sprung up. "If this is the case, then how can we know which is the true church of Isa?" they ask. The short answer is: The true church of Isa is the universal assembly of believers who have held faithfully to His teachings from the beginning. But this answer requires further explanation.

It is helpful to remember that the first followers of Isa were not known as members of some denomination; they were known simply as "disciples," that is, followers or imitators of Isa. Later in Acts 11:26 they were given the name "Christian." The word "Christian" is derived from the Greek word 'Xristos,' meaning Messiah, so the original meaning was 'follower of the Messiah.' The Church belongs to Isa, not to certain people. The true Church follows only Isa al Masih. The Injil stresses that He established this assembly upon the foundation of the prophets and apostles whom He chose Himself.[51]

So how was the Church established? Ten days after Isa ascended to heaven, the disciples and early believers were gathered together in Jerusalem, waiting for the 'parakletos,' the Holy Spirit whom Isa had promised. Suddenly a sound like a powerful wind from heaven filled the place where they met, and everyone was filled with the Holy Spirit. From there they went out to the people and began testifying to the death and

---

51 See: Ephesians 2:20.

resurrection of Isa. The astounding result was that 3,000 people believed in Isa in one day, and the first church was formed.[52] The first believers continued meeting together and shared everything they had with each other. They learned the teaching of Isa from His apostles, and they boldly proclaimed His death and resurrection to all people.

Not long afterwards, they were forced to scatter because the Jewish leaders began killing the Christians. Yet, everywhere they went, new groups of believers, or "churches," sprouted up throughout the Roman Empire and even beyond the borders of the empire. They met in members' homes, in public meeting rooms, or, if necessary, in secret places because of persecution. In spite of all this opposition their numbers grew because of the believers' faith and courage, such that within a mere 300 years there was scarcely anyone left in the empire who had not heard the name of Isa. Thus churches continued to multiply. And yet these scattered Christians did not consist of denominations or organizations. They were simply the universal church of Isa.

In the Injil, the word "church" is used with two senses or meanings: First, what we call the "universal church" consisting of all believers in every place and in every century who truly follow Isa. This group has no boundaries of race, language or nationality. Secondly,

---

[52] Acts 2
[53] See: Romans 1:17; Galatians 2:16; Ephesians 2:8-9.

there is, what we call, the "local church" consisting of an assembly of believers in Isa who live and meet in a particular location for worship, prayer, Bible study, and mutual support. There are millions of local churches across the globe. These people are bound together by their common faith in Isa, but they also live near each other and are similar enough to each other that they can gather together and understand each other for worship, prayer, and teaching.

The teaching about faith is one of the essentials of Christianity. According to the Injil, only sincere faith or belief in the death and resurrection of Isa saves us from our sins and makes us part of His Church.[53] To

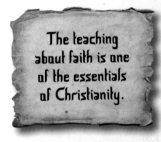

The teaching about faith is one of the essentials of Christianity.

add any other condition to this goes absolutely against the teaching of the Injil. Every person who believes in Isa alone, regardless of nationality or denomination, is a member of His Universal Church.

I do not represent any denomination like Catholic, Orthodox, or Protestant. I am simply a follower of Isa. I need not protest against anyone; I simply seek to proclaim Isa al Masih. I do not believe it is our place or responsibility to determine which people are true Christians. Our responsibility is to embrace God's Word as followers of Isa.

Many may claim to have a special relationship to Isa or to represent Him, and yet there is a story from the life of Isa that tells us who really is on His side. On a certain occasion Isa received news that His mother and brothers were waiting to meet with Him. The Injil records that Isa replied: *"My mother and brothers are those who hear the Word of God and keep it"* (Luke 8:19-21). We can see from this that not even family ties can bring us closer to God; the only way is to believe and obey the Word of God. That is the only true test for knowing who is truly following Isa.

His love and His Spirit continues to bind all true believers worldwide into one family.

So even though there may be any number of different kinds of churches, the important thing is that they all agree that the true head of the Church is none other than Isa al Masih. It is His love and His Spirit that continues to bind all true believers worldwide into one family. Consequently, there is really only one way to know whether or not a local assembly or person is part of the true Church of Isa, that is, to see whether or not they remain true to the entire teaching of the Bible. If they obey God's Word, then they belong to Isa. If a church or denomination abandons this principle, they have wandered away from the biblical example.

Throughout history and to this day countless wrongs have been committed in the name of Christianity. However none of these wrongs have been done according to God's Word. On the contrary they were selfish human acts by people who called themselves Christians and yet did not actually follow Isa and His teachings. These wrongs grieve true Christians deeply, but it is important for people not to misinterpret these actions as representative of true Christianity. For Christians, it is essential that they commit themselves to obeying Isa and His Word.

In conclusion, denominations founded by man are not what really matters in the eyes of God. God looks at the hearts of individuals, not at all the traditions or expensive buildings we might build. What God acknowledges is the universal assembly of believers who remain faithful to Isa by the power of God's Spirit. This unity and harmony is the ongoing miracle of Isa. Today there are thousands of secret followers of Isa, even in the Middle East, who might not be able to openly attend a church. Yet they belong to Isa and they are not alone. Every believer of the Injil and Isa, despite coming from different nationalities, languages, and denominations, is a member of one united and truly universal church.

How Do Christians Worship God?

Like most of my Muslim friends you may be curious to find out how Christians worship God. For Muslims, worship consists of five daily prayers, fasting one month out of the year, giving to the poor, and other religious rites. So you may wonder if the worship of Christians is similar. Many of my Muslim friends think that it must be very easy to be a Christian because they don't have to pray and fast. That is not so; in fact, Christians do both. I should remind you that Mohammed first learned about praying and fasting from the Jews and Christians in Arabia. However, it is important not to define Christianity by its religious practices because, according to the Injil, what is important is not doing certain religious rites, but rather actually having a change of heart and lifestyle as a result of knowing Isa al Masih personally.

What most Muslims see is that Christians attend worship in a church building on Sunday. Most followers of Isa traditionally gather together on Sunday, the day that Isa rose from the dead, to worship God. This is a time to sing hymns of worship, as well as say prayers together to God and also listen to teaching from the Bible.

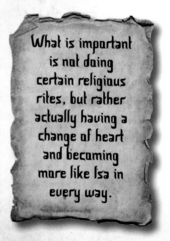

What is important is not doing certain religious rites, but rather actually having a change of heart and becoming more like Isa in every way.

Christians also regularly partake in a very simple symbolic meal of bread and the fruit of the vine as part of their worship because Isa said to remember His death and resurrection in this way. Christians also collect a regular monetary offering so the church can help meet the needs of others. This weekly meeting however is not the end of their worship. For a true follower of Isa, worship is not only something done in church on Sunday but rather a new way of life in response to God's Word and what He has done for them. Believers seek to praise and obey God every day, in every circumstance and with everything they do and say.

> **Believers seek to praise and obey God every day, in every circumstance and with everything they do and say.**

Prayer is essential to the Christian because it is a way to communicate directly with God. Prayer is the believer's way of showing dependence upon God, expressing thanks and adoration, as well as requests for self and others. Isa taught His followers about prayer in this way:

❖ *And when you pray, you must not be like the hypocrites. For they love to stand and pray in the synagogues (Jewish meeting places) and at the street corners, that they may be seen by others. Truly, I say to you, they have received their reward. But when you pray, go into your room and shut the door and pray to your Father who is in secret. And your Father who sees in secret will reward you. And when you pray, do not heap up empty phrases as the Gentiles (Infidels) do, for they think that they will be heard for their many words. Do not be like them, for your Father knows what you need before you ask Him. Pray then like this:*

> *Our Father in heaven,*
> *hallowed be Your name.*
> *Your kingdom come,*
> *Your will be done,*
> *on earth as it is in heaven.*
> *Give us this day our daily bread,*
> *and forgive us our debts,*
> *as we also have forgiven our debtors.*
> *And lead us not into temptation,*
> *but deliver us from evil.*

–Matthew 6:5-13

Isa stressed that God is not interested in our bodily motions or memorized words, but rather He examines our heart's condition. Likewise, Isa encouraged His followers to call God their "Father" and to speak to Him freely. This may surprise you, my Muslim friend, because you are not accustomed to calling God "Father," but that is what Isa taught. He said that God

> Not only is it important to talk with God, but we must also listen to Him.

indeed loves us all like His own children, and He is eager to listen to our cry for help.

Not only is it important to talk with God, but we must also listen to Him. That is why we make time to read God's Word regularly for ourselves. For us, the Injil is not simply a book for scholars to debate or for people to memorize; it is a loving letter from God our Father to each and every one of us His children. This is why Christians should take time to read it every day and listen to their Father's voice and learn more about Him and His perfect will for their lives.

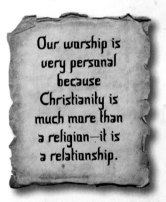

Our worship is very personal because Christianity is much more than a religion—it is a relationship.

Isa also taught His disciples about fasting.[54] However He made it clear that fasting was not a means to get anything from God; rather it is a way for us to humble ourselves before Him. Isa also stressed that the purpose of fasting was not to gain the applause of the people around us. Most importantly, through fasting we are able to focus on a particular need or concern we might have and pray about it without distraction.

---

[54] Matthew 6:16-18.

As can be seen, our worship is very personal because Christianity is much more than a religion—it is a relationship. In religion, people try to do good to gain salvation and God's favor; but in following Isa, the Christian accepts His free gift of salvation and loving favor. This makes the believer want to live in a right and holy relationship with God. So worship is the expression of a close and intimate relationship with our Father God.

Conclusion

All the things we have talked about may be strange and overwhelming for you if you are not familiar with God's Word. Indeed for many of my Muslim friends the concept of having such a close relationship with God is strange and foreign. Maybe for you God has always seemed distant and even eager to punish, yet what we read in the Injil is quite the opposite.

First of all, I would encourage you to understand who God really is and what He thinks of you. In the Injil there is a remarkable verse which summarizes God's character. In 1 John 4:7 it says: *"God is love."* This is a truly amazing statement. It does not simply mean that God loves us in general or that He loves everyone. The verse states that God in His essential nature *is* love. Understanding this simple truth can unlock answers to many questions.

> **1 John 4:7,
> "God is love."**

For example, many people wonder why God created humans to begin with. Many say that God created us to serve and worship Him. That answer doesn't satisfy me completely, because it assumes that God needed or wanted something from us. The fact is that God is totally self-sufficient and we cannot give Him anything He doesn't already have. He is awesome and great whether I worship Him or not. Many of my Muslim friends respond that God created humans in order to test them. Again this response does not satisfy me either because it implies that God does not know everything or that He is in fact just toying with us. So why did God create us?

We can better understand why by considering a real-life illustration. Everywhere in the world people keep having babies. Now when you really think about this, it makes no sense to have babies because when a baby invades your home your life is turned upside down. Yet parents all over the world still persist in having children. Why? Are they expecting to get something out of that child? Hopefully not! Frankly babies are not a very logical investment of our time and money. So why do parents the world over persist in having children? The fact is that parents don't want to *get* something from their children, rather they want to *give* something to them. This is called love.

I believe this helps us understand why God created us. It was not to get something from us. God *needs* nothing. On the contrary He simply wanted to give to us out of His endless love. Just like a mother and father gladly provide for all the needs of their children in hope that one day they will enjoy a happy relationship with them, so God put us in this special world which He created for us because He simply wants to show us

His love. Furthermore, His ultimate desire is that one day each one of us may enjoy a loving relationship with Him. When we look carefully at the first chapters of the Bible we see that God created Adam and Hawwa to be His children, to love and cherish them. He wanted an eternal relationship with them.

However Satan was jealous of God and he decided to ruin God's family. He convinced Adam and Hawwa that they could be happier without God. So they rebelled and ate from the forbidden fruit. Soon they realized what a terrible mistake they had committed. God was then forced to send them away from the Garden of Eden

Although Adam and Hawwa were infected with sin and destined to die, God promised to save them.

because now they were infected with sin and destined to die. Yet at the same time, God promised He would save them. That is how the story of our human race began. God promised that the *"seed of the woman"* would one day defeat Satan.

God gave us this promise immediately after the seed of sin and death was sown into the hearts of mankind when Adam sinned. Many of my Muslim friends think Christians believe that babies are born as sinners. This is misleading. The Bible says that all men and women born after Adam have been born with the seed of sin in them.[55] However it is only as we choose to sin on our own that this seed sprouts and bears evil fruit. It is for this personal sin that God will hold each one of us accountable. It is obvious that everyone sins and everyone dies because the punishment for sin is death.[56] If Adam had not sinned, he never would have died; but the fact that all people die clearly shows that we are all sinners.

The fact that all people die clearly shows that we are all sinners.

Throughout the Tawrat and Zabur, God reached out to mankind through the prophets. He tried to teach them His Laws, but mankind always rebelled. Still God promised to one day send a Savior and win

---

[55] See: Romans 5:12-15.
[56] See: Romans 6:23.

The Injil reminds us that it was God's great love that motivated Him to send a Savior to pay for our sins and spare us from hell.

them back. Finally one day Isa was born to the virgin Maryam. He was the fulfillment of God's promises through the prophets; He was God's loving Word in human flesh. Despite His perfect life, people did not recognize Him as the Savior of the world and they killed Him on the cross. Yet this was God's plan all along because through Isa's death, He paid for all mankind's sin and defeated Satan. Not only that, but He also rose again victorious over death and opened the gates of heaven to all who believe in Him. The Injil reminds us that it was God's great love that motivated Him to send a Savior to pay for our sins and spare us from hell.

❖ *For God so loved the world, that He gave His only Son, that whoever believes in Him should not perish but have eternal life* (John 3:16).

All that God requires is that we believe in the one He sent, Isa. In fact He offers us eternal life in heaven if we simply believe in the Savior, Isa al Masih. Here I must clarify what heaven means in the Injil. Many of my friends have warped ideas about heaven, but the Bible makes it clear that heaven is not a place for selfish pleasure, but rather a place for eternal fellowship with God

Heaven is not a place for selfish pleasure, but rather a place for eternal fellowship with God Himself.

Himself. There believing men and women will live in perfect harmony with God forever (see Revelation chapters 21 & 22). All of this is promised to those who put their full trust in Isa.

Dear Muslim friend, you may believe that you must keep trying to please God with good works in order to earn heaven. The Injil tells us that because we are sinful, it is impossible for us to gain God's favor through our good works.[57] Many believe that their good works will one day be put on a great balance scale and they hope that these will outweigh their bad works. The truth is that our standard for "good" is infinitely inferior to God's perfect standard. Furthermore, our debt to God for our sin is far greater than we could ever pay off with our good works, not to mention that even our best actions are often motivated by selfishness. The fact is that the Injil never speaks of such a balance in the Last Day. Rather it tells us that Isa al Masih will sit on a great white throne to judge every person according to his/her deeds.[58]

---

[57] See: Ephesians 2:8-9
[58] See: Revelation 20:11-15.
[59] See: James 2:10.
[60] See: Romans 3:23.

Again many think that by working hard to keep God's laws they can somehow gain His favor and forgiveness. However, we forget that just doing one wrong deed means that we have broken God's perfect Law.[59] Not only that, but doing something right does not erase the wrong we have done or gain us special favor with God. Suppose someone is very careful not to break any traffic laws for a whole week, then they go into the police station and seek a reward because they broke no laws that week. What kind of reaction would they get? The police would laugh at them. Obviously laws are not designed to reward good behavior but to punish wrong actions. It is the same with God's holy Law.

In the beginning God created mankind perfect. He designed us to do good. We cannot expect God to reward us for doing what we were created to do. However, we can be certain that His law will punish us for the evil we have done. The Bible says that our sins have separated us from God, and that one day He will have to punish

It is important to accept God's free gift of salvation.

us for all our evil deeds.[60] This punishment will be eternal separation from God, namely the eternal fires of hell. Many people are hoping that this punishment will be only temporary. Yet Isa Himself made it clear that hell is eternal: *"Where their worm does not die, and the fire is not quenched"* (Mark 9:48).

That is why it is so important that we accept God's free gift of salvation. He sent Isa specifically to take the punishment for our sins on the cross. God did this because He knew that we could not be saved by our own efforts. Isa al Masih was God's perfect sacrifice for all our sins. All we need to do is accept His offer of salvation by believing in the Lamb of God Isa. It is only by His great sacrifice that we can have freedom from our sin and hope of eternal life with God. For it is not our good works that save us, rather the great work of Isa al Masih on the cross is the only way for us to be saved.

Many of my Muslim friends struggle in understanding how the death of one man could bring life to all mankind. They, and perhaps you, believe that one man cannot bear the punishment of another. However in real life this happens all the time. If my son breaks someone's window, who pays to have it replaced? I do. If my son goes to prison, who pays his fine to get him out? I do. The reality is that our debt to God for all our sins is so great that we could never pay Him. That is why God through Isa paid our debt so we could be free. He did this simply because He, like a true Father, loves us.

Isa told a beautiful story that illustrates our rebellion toward God and His undying love toward us:

❖ *And He said, "There was a man who had two sons. And the younger of them said to his father, 'Father, give me the share of property that is coming to me.' And he divided his* property between them. Not many days later, the younger son gathered all he had and took a journey into a far country, and there he squandered his property in reckless living. And when he had spent everything, a severe famine arose in that country, and he began to be in need. So he went and hired himself out to one of the citizens of that country, who sent him into his fields to feed pigs. And he was longing to be fed with the pods that the pigs ate, and no one gave him anything. But when he came to himself, he said, 'How many of my father's hired servants have more than enough bread, but I perish here with hunger! I will arise and go to my father, and I will say to him, Father, I have sinned against heaven and before you. I am no longer worthy to be called your son. Treat me as one of your hired servants.' And he arose and came to his father. But while he was still a long way off, his father saw him and felt compassion, and ran and embraced him and kissed him. And the son said to him, 'Father, I have sinned against heaven and before you. I am no longer worthy to be called your son.' But the father said to his servants, 'Bring quickly the best robe, and put it on him, and put a ring on his hand, and shoes on his feet. And bring the fattened calf and kill it, and let us eat and celebrate. For this my son was dead, and is alive again; he was lost, and is found.' And they began to celebrate. Now his older son was in the field, and as he came and drew near to the house, he heard music and dancing. And he called one of the servants and asked what these things meant. And he said to him, 'Your brother has come, and your father has killed the fattened calf, because he has received him back safe and sound.' But he was angry and refused to go in. His father came out and entreated him, but he answered his father, 'Look, these many years I have served you, and I never disobeyed your command, yet you never gave me a young goat, that I might celebrate with my friends. But when this son of

"His father saw him and felt compassion, and ran and embraced him and kissed him."

yours came, who has devoured your property with prostitutes, you killed the fattened calf for him!' And he said to him, 'Son, you are always with me, and all that is mine is yours. It was fitting to celebrate and be glad, for this your brother was dead, and is alive; he was lost, and is found'" (Luke 15:11-32).

God is waiting for us to repent and return home to be part of His family again.

In this story, the father symbolizes God and his two sons are mankind. What the younger son did was selfish and shameful. He essentially told his father that he wished his father would hurry up and die. Then he took the money of the inheritance his father gave him and spent it for his own pleasure. Soon he was alone and miserable. He became so hungry he even desired the food of pigs. Only then did he realize his terrible mistake and returned to his father's home. He surely expected his father to beat him. How surprised he must have been to find that his father was waiting for him. The father ran out to meet him, embraced him, and accepted him again as his son. The younger son is a picture of how so many of us have wasted the life that God has given us. We think that God will not want us anymore. Yet God is waiting for us to repent and return home to be part of His family again.

What about the older son? He is a picture of those among us who are religious and think we deserve special favors from God. He was living close to the father and yet in his heart he was further away than his younger brother. He was proud and arrogant. In reality he was in worse condition than his younger brother because he did not know the love of his father. Sadly many people think that being religious and working very hard to please God will earn them a special place in heaven. They are wrong. What God desires is a humble heart. He wants genuine repentance. He desires a sincere relationship based on love, not duty.

God desires a sincere relationship based on love, not duty.

This is exactly what the Injil teaches. All of us have rebelled and run far away from our Father. Yet He is eager to welcome us home. Not only does God want to forgive us our sins, but through Isa He wants to bring us close to Himself again so that we can once again be His children as Adam and Hawwa were. He wants us all to be part of His family once more. The Injil says:

❖ *But to all who did receive Him, who believed in His name, He gave the right to become children of God, who were born, not of blood nor of the will of the flesh nor of the will of man, but of God* (John 1:12-13).

God is inviting every one of us into a deep and personal relationship with Himself. This relationship is one that begins in this life on earth but also one that will last forever. He promises us eternal life with Him in His glorious home. Dear Muslim friend, you may believe it is impossible to know for sure that we will be saved. You may think that anyone who says they are sure that they will be saved is arrogant and foolish. However I believe we can be sure, based on God's invitation and promise, not on our own good works. You see, because God has provided a way to be forgiven, He can also guarantee our salvation. God's Word says:

❖ *If you confess with your mouth that Jesus [Isa] is Lord and believe in your heart that God raised Him from the dead, you will be saved* (Romans 10:9).

If you sincerely put your trust in Isa, God promises to forgive your sins and give you eternal life with Him in heaven.

My dear Muslim friend, you must remember that the differences that now divide mankind (confusion about religions and misinformation about the truth) were not created by God, but rather by Satan. God is one and He wants us all to be one family with Him forever. In

---

[61] See: 1 Timothy 2:5-6.

the Bible God has shown the only way for all mankind to be saved.[61] Isa al Masih said it Himself:

❖ *I am the Way the Truth and the Life. No one comes to the Father except by Me* (John 14:6).

Dear friend, if you are seeking the truth about God and the way to eternal life, then you desperately need to know Isa al Masih. He is alive today and if you cry out to Him, He will show you the way to God. In order to be forgiven, all you must do is choose to believe in the truth that Isa al Masih is the Savior whom God promised to send to mankind, and that Isa died for your sins and rose again. If you sincerely put your trust in Isa, God promises to forgive your sins and give you eternal life with Him in heaven.

Notes

Keep Discovering & Learning

One God One Message
by P. D. Bramsen

Weaving together real-life stories and emails from Muslims around the world, this unhurried journey through the best story ever told gives seekers, skeptics, Muslims, and confused Christians the chance to overcome countless obstacles and arrive at a clear conclusion about the one true God and His consistent message.

Available at www.one-god-one-message.com

One God, One Way
by Kevin G. Dyer

In a famous European palace, visitors can find a maze made out of hedges. It is easy to get lost in that maze, but not so easy to find the only way out. Life is like that maze. There are many confusing paths to take. How can we know the right way—the one true way to the one true God? This study will help you find that One Way.

Available at www.ecsministries.org